# Soul-Searching the Church:
## Free Methodism at 150 Years

Gerald E. Bates and Howard A. Snyder, editors

*Reflections on the*
"Search for the Free Methodist Soul"

*Sponsored by the*
Committee on Free Methodist History & Archives
Marston Memorial Historical Center

Soul-Searching the Church: Free Methodism at 150 Years
Reflections on the "Search for the Free Methodist Soul"

Gerald E. Bates and Howard A. Snyder, editors
Regine Stotts, cover design

Pictured on cover: (front) Rachel Bradley, E.P. Hart, Polly Ho, José Ildo Swartele de Mello, Jennifer Starr-Reivitt, B.T. Roberts, Mark Van Valin, (back) Jeanne Acheson-Munos, Gerald Bates, Henry Church, Doug Newton

All scripture quotations, unless otherwise indicated, are taken from the HOLY BIBLE, TODAY'S NEW INTERNATIONAL VERSION®. TNIV®. Copyright © 2001, 2005 by International Bible Society. Used by permission of Zondervan. All rights reserved.

All rights reserved. No part of this book may be reproduced in any form, except for brief quotations in reviews, without the written permission of the Marston Memorial Historical Center.

ISBN 0-89367-288-2

Copyright © 2007 by
Marston Memorial Historical Center

Committee on Free Methodist History & Archives
Free Methodist Historical Society
Marston Memorial Historical Center

Free Methodist World Ministries Center
770 N. High School Road, Indianapolis, IN 46253-5002
Email: History@fmcna.org

Printed in the United States of America
print on demand by Light and Life Communications
Indianapolis, IN 46214

*In Tribute to*

# Betty Carolyn Shipley
(1938-2000)

This book is published in memory of Betty Carolyn Shipley, a committed Christian servant and a longtime friend of the Marston Memorial Historical Center. The book's publication has been facilitated by the Betty Shipley Memorial Fund.

Betty Carolyn Shipley grew up in a parsonage where the idea of a calling to a life of ministry wasn't anything new. When Betty first felt God's call to Christian ministry in the Free Methodist Church, she said, "I can't preach like my brothers, I can't sing like my sisters, but I could work in an office."

Just a few months before completing her college degree, she saw an ad in *The Free Methodist* magazine for someone to work in the Servicemen's Department at Free Methodist Headquarters in Indiana. Rather than quit so close to finishing the course, Betty decided to complete her studies. When after graduation she discovered that the job had not been filled, she saw God's direction and went to Winona Lake, Indiana, where she began her life of ministry in late 1960 at $1.00 per hour!

Preserving Free Methodist history was a life-long concern for Betty Shipley. She served the church in many ways, a faithful worker in the Free Methodist Church from 1960 until her death in 2000. She also served at Seattle Pacific University, as a VISA missionary in Africa, at the Southern California Conference Office, in addition to working in several departments at the World Ministries Center in both Winona Lake and Indianapolis. Finally she served at the Deaconess Foundation in Oklahoma City, Oklahoma.

Betty loved serving the Lord in her church. Serving as

Jesus did was a major focus in her life and she brought a spirit of kindness, gentleness and quiet strength to each task. She was determined to fulfill her calling to the end.

Friends of Betty established the Betty Shipley Memorial Fund through the Free Methodist Foundation to honor her life and faithfulness to the church and to extend the ministry of the Marston Memorial Historical Center.

# Contents

| | Introduction | Gerald Bates and Howard Snyder | 7 |

Chapter

1. Tell the Story: The Soul Importance of Free Methodist History
   *Editor Doug Newton* — 13
2. Free Methodist Trajectories: The Road We Took
   *Stan Ingersol* — 27
3. Growing Up Free Methodist
   *Pastor Linda Adams* — 43
4. Embodying Our Mission
   *Pastor Mark Van Valin* — 55
5. Learning from Brazilian Free Methodism
   *Bishop José Ildo Swartele de Mello* — 69
6. Free Methodist Mission: Justice
   *Pastor John Hay* — 81
7. Free Methodist Mission: Mercy
   *Pastor Henry Church* — 101
8. Free Methodist Mission: Truth
   *U. Milo Kaufmann* — 111
9. Reflections and Reactions
   *Comments from Participants* — 127
10. Seven Keys to Free Methodist Renewal
    *Howard Snyder* — 137
11. The Free Methodist Soul: Did We Find It?
    *Bishop Emeritus Gerald Bates* — 159
12. Our Calling to the Poor
    *Bishop Joseph James* — 163

Study Guide  *Chapter discussion questions*  181

*Introduction*
# The Search for the Free Methodist Soul

### Gerald Bates and Howard Snyder

In 2003 the Committee on Free Methodist History and Archives projected three open-ended symposiums focusing on the theme, "Search for the Free Methodist Soul." These gatherings occurred in Indianapolis in March of 2004, 2005, and 2006. The aim of the conversations was to help fulfill the Marston Memorial Historical Center's mission "to preserve Free Methodist heritage and transmit it faithfully to each generation in order to assist the Free Methodist Church in fulfilling its mission."

Total attendance for the three events was 237, and others participated indirectly via email and through papers that were circulated. Attendance at the three events averaged about eighty; the first was the smallest and the third was the largest.

This book makes the fruit of the three symposiums more widely available. Included here are most of the papers presented at the gatherings, plus additional reflections and comments. *Note* that we have added also, as chapter twelve, Bishop Joseph James important sermon at the 2007 General Conference, "Our Calling to the Poor." This passionate plea makes a key contribution to the book.

### Why Search? Why Soul?

"The Free Methodist Church again seeks to define its soul, articulate its mission, respond to its origin and seek a fresh understanding of God's purpose for this day," wrote John Van Valin in his Foreword to *A Future with a History: The Wesleyan Witness of the Free Methodist Church,* by David L. McKenna (Light and Life Communications, 1997). This was the spirit of the three Search events.

As explained in the call to the first symposium, the gatherings were focused as follows:

PURPOSE: To stimulate reflection on and renewed commitment to the identity and mission of the Free Methodist Church.

RATIONALE: The Committee on Free Methodist History and Archives became increasingly aware of a buzz of concern and interest across the church about Free Methodist identity today. We wanted to provide a place and time where we could worship, pray, and share our ideas and insights. We envisioned simply a conversation — no declarations, resolutions, or proposed action. What might the Holy Spirit do if interested people met to think and pray about the life and vitality of the Free Methodist soul?

INVITATION: We welcomed all interested Free Methodists, especially those for whom this question struck a deep chord. We wanted to bridge the generations — young and old, and those in between. We felt wisdom was found in intergenerational dialogue.

OBJECTIVES:
1. Celebrate the witness of the Free Methodist Church, past and present.
2. Explore honestly the contours of FM identity — the pluses and minuses; what we have done well; where we have failed; what we can learn.
3. Seek God's face for a fresh touch of his Holy Spirit.
4. Learn from one another's stories.
5. Renew our commitment to God's work through the Free Methodist Church.
6. Provide insights that will help the Historical Center in developing its ongoing work.

## The Three Symposiums

The first and third symposiums were held at the Free Methodist World Ministries Center in Indianapolis; the second at the facilities of the Indianapolis West Morris Street Free Methodist Church. All three gatherings met Monday afternoon and evening and until noon on Tuesday.

**2004 Symposium, March 22-23.** The symposium opened with worship and a meditation by Bishop Joe James. Bishop Les Krober gave a meditation on Tuesday morning. Plenary presentations were made by *Light and Life* editor Doug Newton, Church of the Nazarene archivist and historian Stan Ingersol, and Pastor Linda Adams of the New Hope Free Methodist Church, Rochester, New York. Their papers are included in this book. Responses to the presentations were given by Jennifer Starr-Reivitt, Jon Kulaga, and Bob Cannon. The moderator was Bishop Emeritus Gerald Bates. The program included plenary and small-group discussion, question-and-answer time with a panel of presenters and respondents, a findings report, and concluding comments by Howard Snyder.

**2005 Symposium, March 14-15.** This gathering focused on global, not just North American, Free Methodism. After worship and a meditation by Helen Kaufmann, Bishop José Ildo Mello presented insights and a challenge from the perspective of the Free Methodist Church in Brazil. Other major presentations were given by Pastor Mark Van Valin (Spring Arbor, Michigan), and Polly Ho, Free Methodist missions leader in Asia. Responses came from Dwight Gregory, Alma Cordova, and Thad Roller, all of whom have been active in ethnic or cross-cultural church planting. The symposium again included a panel, discussion in small groups and in general sessions, and reflections by Howard Snyder. The papers presented by Bishop José Ildo and Pastor Mark Van Valin are included in this book.

**2006 Symposium, March 13-14.** This symposium was organized around "Justice, Mercy, and Truth" — a phrase common in John Wesley's writings. Gerry Coates, executive director of Free Methodist Communications, served as moderator and Eric Spangler led the worship times.

Major presentations were given by Pastor John Hay of the Indianapolis West Morris Street Church (justice), Africa Missions Area Director Henry Church (mercy), and U. Milo Kaufmann (truth). All are included in this book. Respondents were Jeanne Acheson-Munos, Bonnie Brann, and Gerald Bates. This time there were longer periods of open discussion rather than small-group sessions.

**Overview of This Book**

The twelve chapters in this book present eight of the symposium plenary papers, a summary of reflections and feedback, reflective chapters by the editors of this volume, and Joseph James' call to ministry with the poor.

The Committee on Free Methodist History and Archives felt it was essential to make this material available to the wider church. Frankly, we think the eight symposium essays included here are too insightful — and too important — to be lost in the mists of one-time events. Some of the contributions to this book are not only timely; they're timeless, especially those that help us better understand our history internally and in relation to the larger church.

There is something here for everyone — stories, history, philosophical discussion, humor, personal testimony, theology. Some chapters may make you smile or weep; others you may find puzzling or challenging. But they are all part of the picture, all pieces in the puzzle of Free Methodism today.

Readers will see (unsurprisingly) that the contributors don't all agree on just what the "Free Methodist soul" is, let alone on what is needed to spark greater vitality and more effective mission. Yet they all contribute something important. At the end of the book we attempt to point some directions.

The first three chapters, from the first symposium, are foundational. They help us understand our roots and character. Doug Newton shows why it is important for Free Methodists continually to rehearse their story as the horizon of history constantly recedes. Stan Ingersol, an accomplished historian of the holiness movement, provides key insights both on the origin of the Free Methodist Church and on influences that shaped us at different stages in our history. Linda Adams helps bring the story up to date by relating her own FM history since the 1960s.

Chapters four and five, by Pastor Mark Van Valin and Bishop José Ildo, highlight the challenge of Free Methodist mission today in light of our heritage. Mark has pastored urban churches in St. Louis and Indianapolis and shows particular sensitivity to issues of compassionate justice and ministry with the poor. Bishop Ildo speaks from the context of dynamic movemental Free Methodism in Brazil. He draws upon the experience of the Brazilian church and also challenges us anew with our heritage from John Wesley and early Methodism.

Chapters six, seven, and eight come from the third symposium, organized around the themes of justice, mercy, and truth. When John Wesley spoke of holy living in the world, he often used the phrase *justice, mercy, and truth* as a summary of Christian ethics, holiness lived in society. Through this threefold theme the 2006 symposium explored our history and sought insights for mission today. John Hay provides a significant essay on the missional meaning of *justice*, and Henry Church shows how *mercy* is being expressed through Free Methodist work in Africa. Milo Kaufmann, employing some postmodern irony, deals with the contentious issue of *truth*.

Chapter nine gathers up responses and comments from the three symposiums and some additional feedback.

In chapter ten, Howard Snyder reflects on the whole "Search" process in light of Free Methodist history and identity and offers seven suggestions for denominational renewal. Chapter eleven, by Gerald Bates, reflects on the ways the three "Search" events did help us discern the Free Methodist soul. The book fittingly concludes with Bishop James' sermon, which has been left largely in sermonic form (and is also being published separately as a booklet by Light & Life Communications).

We also provide a Study Guide of discussion questions on each chapter. This can be used in classes or small groups, or for personal reflection, as an aid in exploring the issues raised here.

## CHAPTER 1
# Tell the Story: The Soul Importance of Free Methodist History

Doug Newton
Editor, *Light and Life* Magazine

They say history repeats itself. Yet they also say that movements can't be reborn once the movement has hardened into an institution. I wish "they" would decide which it is.

Is history cyclical — can it be repeated? Or is it linear, straight-line — can movements not be renewed? Can the passion and genius of the first fifty years of our history be a revived? Or have we moved beyond any hope of ever being a movement again?

I think there's a chance for renewed momentum. But if it's ever to be the case, we must pay attention to history's lessons. Let's examine those lessons through the lens of my own history as a fourth generation Free Methodist.

**Lesson #1: History does not repeat itself; people repeat it.**

During my student years at Roberts Wesleyan College, I was permanently influenced by an old scholar, G. Ernest Wright, whose book on the Old Testament, *God Who Acts* called my attention to the concept of "theology as recital." I don't know if he coined the idea, and I am not sure that his use of the concept as a systematic construct for biblical criticism wasn't overreaching. But this construct for understanding the Bible persuaded me that for a religious community to perpetuate identity and mission there must be a collective commitment to the recital of its history. The admonitions and warnings found explicitly stated in Psalm 78 draw a one-to-one correspondence between recital and community continuity.

> PS 78:1 O my people, hear my teaching;
> listen to the words of my mouth.

> ² I will open my mouth in parables,
>     I will utter hidden things, things from of old —
> ³ what we have heard and known,
>     what our fathers have told us.
> ⁴ We will not hide them from their children;
>     we will tell the next generation
>   the praiseworthy deeds of the LORD,
>     his power, and the wonders he has done.
> ⁵ He decreed statutes for Jacob
>     and established the law in Israel,
>   which he commanded our forefathers
>     to teach their children,
> ⁶ so the next generation would know them,
>     even the children yet to be born,
>     and they in turn would tell their children.
> ⁷ Then they would put their trust in God
>     and would not forget his deeds
>     but would keep his commands.
> ⁸ They would not be like their forefathers —
>     a stubborn and rebellious generation,
>   whose hearts were not loyal to God,
>     whose spirits were not faithful to him.
> ⁹ The men of Ephraim, though armed with bows,
>     turned back on the day of battle;
> ¹⁰ they did not keep God's covenant
>     and refused to live by his law.
> ¹¹ They forgot what he had done,
>     the wonders he had shown them.

The word "then" in verse 7 is the hinge point of the if-then argument which can be simply stated, "If through faithful recitation one generation will pass on to the next the things they know of God through oral transmission and experience, *then* succeeding generations will continue in faithful covenant with God."

Now it may seem enlightened to take issue with such a simplistic one-to-one correspondence between recital and community faithfulness and continuity, but is it? And while there may be other factors that contribute to an unsuccessful transference of community identity and mission, I would place my bet on recital as the *sine qua non* — the "that without which there is nothing" — of continuity.

When a community fails in recital it fails in continuity.

♦ ♦ ♦ ♦ ♦

I grew up in the quintessential Free Methodist church. It was one of the cookie cutter churches built in the 1960s with exposed arch beams in the sanctuary — you know the one I'm talking about. It was as prolific in Free Methodism as McDonalds in America.

We had JMS, CYC, WMS, and VBS, and almost every other three-letter acronym known to man, and my mother was in charge of them all on the familiar two-year rotation that wore out most of our saints who eventually wandered off to the verdant pastures in Gerry or Lakeland or Spring Arbor or Warm Beach. Today we talk about people serving in their "area of giftedness." If someone had talked like that 40 years ago in my home church, everyone would have laughed. What an unrealistic luxury! Spiritual gift inventories? What planet did you come from? The *Planet of the Big Churches*? The only inventorying that went on was asking the questions, "How long has it been since Jeannette took her turn directing CYC?" and "Do you think it's too much to ask Fred to be delegate, trustee, treasurer and a Sunday school teacher — for the next 50 years?" Spiritual gift inventories are to small churches as Disneyworld vacations are to inner-city families.

We had four kids in our youth group when I was in high school, a youth group hosted by the pastor's wife whom we figured was somewhere between 45 and 110 years old — we couldn't tell. We met on Sunday nights, and our group meeting consisted of reading something about a missionary family and having a Bible lesson. Amazing that nearly everyone in the various youth groups during that decade is now in ministry or lay leadership!

We had a Bible Quiz team, quarterly communion services, an organ and a piano and a choir that managed to pull off an annual Easter cantata without breaking any windows with the shrill sound of untrained overly-vibrato-ed sopranos and perennially understaffed men's sections — which is to say we had two tenors, one bass who could hear his part and two others who followed usually about a half beat behind and a quartertone flat.

We even had our one rich family who were denominationally connected, due to the husband being on the Board of Administration. This was my early education in the correspondence between wealth, privilege and power. But then every typical Free Methodist church had their rich family who held positions in higher up places that kept us connected with "the denomination."

My family was well-off ourselves though. I remember how bad I felt — my best friend being the pastor's son — knowing that my dad made $20,000 a year, and the pastor's family made $6,500. As I said, this was the quintessential Free Methodist church. Exposed beams. Overworked moms and dads. One rich family. And an under-supported pastor's family.

I suppose its one anomaly was that the pastor wore vestments (a FM oxymoron) and also road motorcycles, played jazz trombone (definitely oxymoronic!) and sported the only evidence of a post-war syndrome I knew about in those days — called a tattoo — that sometimes showed itself when he gestured broadly during some particularly poignant point in his sermons.

But my home church never recited history. We had no liturgies of community memory. The only recital event that comes to mind occurred during our quarterly communion as we used the prescribed service from the *Book of Discipline*.

But there was no Free Methodist history. The most I knew about Roberts or Fairbairn was that one was the founder and the other a bishop, and both were award pins I could earn as a top achiever in CYC.

But there was nothing about a gospel to the poor, or the manifestations of the Holy Spirit, or social advocacy and political action. Don't get me wrong; now that I look back, these influences were felt, but no recitation was heard. And I was left floundering to find the identity of the Free Methodist church on my own. And I found one. Unfortunately, it wasn't very accurate. This leads me to the second lesson we need to learn about history.

To borrow a teaching method with a familiar ring: You have heard how it is said, "Nature abhors a vacuum." But I tell you ...

## Lesson #2: History Abhors a Vacuum

In the absence of formal recital, history will make up its own story. It will not leave the past without a voice. The question always is: *What story will be heard?*

I had been pastoring a Free Methodist church for about three years, long enough to begin building my list of "frequently asked questions" about Free Methodism. Near the top of the list was the perennial, "What's the difference between Free Methodists and regular Methodists?" I had my answer of course, but I wasn't always the one being asked. Sometimes people asked members of my congregation.

In one memorable case, a young couple who had recently become Christians after attending our church, asked one of our older members that question. Ironically, this 75 year old was named Mrs. Younger. Bill and Jean would often pick her up for church. When they had been coming long enough to catch on to the fact that the "Free" in our name referred to a category of Methodists, not just a local designation, like Living Water Methodist or St. Luke's Methodist, they asked Mrs. Younger the question about the difference. Gratefully, they kept coming back to church even after her straightforward, didn't-bat-an-eyelash answer that the difference between Methodists and Free Methodists is that "we believe we don't sin."

I think my official theological response when I heard that answer was "Yikes!"

Over the years my reaction has changed from one of shock to understanding. I came to realize that historical-theological understanding in the church is stratified. In the upper levels of historical-theological conversation people engage in fully formed dialogue on issues like entire sanctification. There may be and most likely always will be disagreement on the finer points of these issues, but at least everyone involved is fully apprised of the breadth of the conversation.

But there are other levels of understanding where people are not privy to the entire conversation. They hear bits and pieces. They hear a camp meeting evangelist preach one sweaty sermon about God's power to utterly transform the human heart; they study an Aldersgate lesson once every four years as the curriculum cycles around to the doctrine of entire sanctification; and these people are left to form their historical-theological opinions around scant input and "sound bites." This is not nearly enough information to come to a mature understanding of our beliefs as Free Methodists, but they don't know that. And history and theology will not lie unformed.

Just as water vapor forms around random dust particles in the air, perceptions of history will form around bits and pieces of random information. And the result is not very often something that can be called showers of blessing — rather more like showers of blunder.

*We believe we don't sin.* Actually, Mrs. Younger's rendition of our historical doctrine is not that far removed from one still extant today in some Free Methodist circles. Recently a Free Methodist pastor, now a superintendent, told me that he was reprimanded by a parishioner for having communion too frequently because "we as Free Methodists should not be put in a position of having to confess sin, since it is contrary to our doctrine of entire sanctification."

History must be intentionally and carefully recited throughout all levels of the church because, like it or not, history is always being recited by someone somewhere. It is our failure to understand these things — namely, that the transmission of history never stops being a matter of oral tradition; that we don't control the promulgation of history just by discussing it academically or writing it down competently; that even in literary cultures history is still largely a function of verbal

> History must be intentionally and carefully recited throughout all levels of the church because, like it or not, history is always being recited by someone somewhere.

transmission by untrained persons — it is our failure to understand these facts that gives rise to the distortion of history and mutation of ideas that ultimately undermine a people's sense of identity and mission.

History abhors a vacuum. History will be heard. But left to itself, left to the natural forces of the mnemonic realm (please note I did not say demonic) it will be heard with little resemblance to the truth. It will be at best a caricature of the truth. And its quaint oddities will have little power to compel the devotion of new generations.

This leads to lesson number three and one example of what I mean by the "natural forces of the mnemonic realm."

**Lesson #3: History Recedes From View Along a Curve**
Margie and I had the privilege of living in heaven on earth, Estes Park, Colorado. Before moving there in the year 2000, we had visited on numerous occasions to camp in the Rockies with our daughters for a vacation. Invariably, we had at most a week to enjoy the breathtaking grandeur of the mountains, and then the day always came when we had to pack up the tent to head home. It became my habit as we drove away to keep one eye on the road ahead and one on the rear view mirror. Like a heart attack victim clinging to life, I did not want my view of the mountains to come to an end. Of course it always did. The distance and curvature of the earth saw to it. There came a point when, like the setting of the sun, the last mountain peak once towering in plain sight shrank and sank below the flat line horizon.

Our view of history is like that. Great moments in time happen. Monumental events shape the lives of thousands. Towering personalities inspire multitudes of people. But the past and the future lie on a curve; our present lives move across the broad circumference of time toward new peaks just coming into view ahead while the old peaks recede.

Call this *the curvature phenomenon of memory*. We have all experienced it in our family histories. To demonstrate this fact, let me lead you through a simple exercise. Imagine yourself standing on the floor. Now begin to think of everything you know about your father or mother. Imagine yourself stacking one fact on another, like building blocks. Where were they born? When? What did they do in school? What was their first job? How did your parents meet? What did they enjoy? Once you begin stacking up facts about your folks you begin to see just how tall this pile of information becomes. Imagine exhausting everything you know about them. The stack of facts is huge.

Now move to the left of that stack of knowledge, as if moving along a timeline toward the preceding generation and begin to stack up everything you know about your grandparents. Imagine exhausting everything you know about them. How tall is that stack. It's much, much smaller than the stack of knowledge about your parents. Now move to the left again,

**The Curvature Phenomenon of Memory**
(present to past: Parents, grandparents, great-grandparents)

*Gray area represents "out of sight/memory."

further into the past, and begin to stack everything you know about your great grandparents. Do you even know their first names? How tall is the stack? Not very tall.

In reality each person's stack of information should be roughly the same height, because they each had equivalent facts about their lives. However, your knowledge of them shrinks, because most of the facts of their lives sink below the horizon of memory due to this curvature phenomenon.

To those of us currently alive, it can seem almost a mocking indignity that our entire lives, for example my life, may be shrunk within just three short generations to a caricatured one-liner: *Great Grandpa Newton used to be a writer of some sort.* Only the highest peaks of my life will be remembered, if at all. And if at all, the scant amount of facts falsifies memory and distorts the truth.

The only way to circumvent the curvature phenomenon is to record a heavily detailed history and inspire some passion in the succeeding generations to read and tell the fuller story of Doug Newton. That is unlikely to happen with me as an individual person, but if it doesn't happen with a whole community of people, there will be a far greater loss of meaning, significance and identity.

The work of the historian is to reach back into the past and counteract the curvature.

My wife and I have done that with the mountains we recently left behind. Photographs, paintings, and artifacts as reminders and even facsimiles of our experiences in the mountains adorn our present home. We stack them high; we compensate for the curvature that removes them from sight by intentional *re*collections that make the distant mountains much more present to us.

Without the work of passionate historians to assemble voluminous records, to stack fact upon fact, to create and safeguard intentional *re*collections, the truth of the past slips from sight taking with it a community's sense of identity and mission. Then after that, token recitals of history, if any, resemble the efforts of an old movie star with a bad facelift trying to look young and beautiful again.

The curvature phenomenon is overcome only by aggressive collection and *re*collection of *all* the facts.

Finally, I must underscore this with one more history lesson.

## Lesson #4: True Recital Forms the Interpretive Lens for the Details of History

To be sure, history is not merely an encyclopedic collection of facts, but the organization of those facts into categories and stories that create context. In that sense, recital is reflexive. It is history serving history. It is history made memorable for the sake of history made clear.

Even as we engage in this symposium the world is presently engaged in a discussion about Mel Gibson's portrayal of the crucifixion in the stirring movie, *The Passion of the Christ*. We have been witnessing first hand how varying contexts of faith elicit widely varied interpretations of the facts of Jesus' death. Numerous groups approach the same set of facts with different faith recitations, and they consequently are repulsed, or angered, or broken, or attracted by what they see.

Then there are those who come with no prior faith recitation. Mel Gibson hopes that his faith which guides the camera, the sounds, and the actors will provide an interpretative context for the facts that leads those viewers to understand Jesus' earthshaking act of sacrificial love. The faith context shapes the perception of facts.

But what if a person is left to observe facts with no context for understanding them? What if there is no recital that creates context?

I grew up in the camp-meeting sect of the Free Methodist church. I never missed one Adam's Center camp meeting from the year I was born until I went to college. Other than quarterly communion, and infrequent reminiscences by my grandparents and parents, I had no connection to our denominational history outside of camp meeting. But in camp meeting history came alive — which is to say, the old people went on display. Wrinkled images of Free Methodism of days gone by.

Camp meeting was an annual unfocused Hubble telescope taking me back in time toward the big bang of the Free Methodist movement. But it never got me all the way back. I could only guess at who we were originally meant to be. And the guess was quite poor.

The uncontextualized images and impressions were all I had to go on to understand our identity and mission as Free Methodists. Images and impressions such as:

- Sister Jones — no please don't let it happen again this year! — getting blessed and running around the tabernacle shouting, "Glory! Glory! Glory!" in tones that made Edith Bunker's voice sound as silky as Sarah Vaughn. She became my visual definition of "being filled with the Holy Spirit."

- Holiness was old people who never loosened their tie, opened their white-shirt collar, or rolled up their sleeves on a hot August Sunday afternoon, because "it was Sunday."

Don't get me wrong. I love how the church shaped me. For example, I'd be willing to bet that my exposure to mellifluous phrases like "superfluous adornment" birthed my love for language. After all, how many children ever hear the word "superfluous" intoned so frequently and reverently before the age of accountability?

As an adult, I came to recognize many other better images of our identity and mission which silently shaped my young heart and mind.

For example, I now recognize that being Free Methodist meant accepting an invitation to dinner at the home of a destitute family who put shaved ice in the milk to keep it cold, because they were too poor to have a good fridge.

It meant choosing as my best friend one of only two black students in my huge high school, because my little Free Methodist church had a black family who had been accepted and loved as people.

It meant my mom standing at a kitchen counter every Wednesday night cutting out construction paper getting ready for CYC because "somebody's got to do it this year."

It meant smelling the smell of padded pews, because when CYC was over for the summer, we went to Wednesday night prayer meeting where they knelt when we prayed.

It meant the irrelevance and inconceivability of asking the question, "What does the church have to offer my kids?"

It meant loyalty, devotion, and lifelong commitment to something much more important than my wishes, my likes and dislikes.

It meant being imprinted about the reality of God by my third grade Sunday School teacher who couldn't teach a lick, or do a thing to hold our attention except cry every time she said the name of Jesus.

Unfortunately, these things were never gathered up and understood in context. And I never saw where the kneeling came from, or tenderness toward the poor ... or why my teacher puddled up at the name of Jesus. I just didn't know, until somebody recited our true history to me. Until someone risked irrelevance — the classic prejudicial charge against all historians — and loved the God of this church enough to say out loud what He had done for the world by raising us up.

> I will utter hidden things, things from of old —
> ³ what we have heard and known,
>   what our fathers have told us.
> ⁴ We will not hide them from their children;
>   we will tell the next generation
>   the praiseworthy deeds of the LORD,
>   his power, and the wonders he has done. (Psalm 78)

There are people who scoff at efforts to keep history alive, to keep the story of history true to history. There are people who would just as soon move on to what's new and let history drop below the horizon. There are such people. But when they are gone both their name and their people will be forgotten.

But as for me, when I am gone and the knowledge of who I was recedes along the curvature of memory and my name is only ink on a family tree, I will have been part of a people raised up by God for making holy history and lasting impressions on the earth. And that's a history worth reciting.

### Five Proposals for Becoming A Recital Church

1. **Make a careful review of FM mutations of historical and doctrinal fact** both by the "tradition-bound" and the "contemporary-relevance" sects of the church.

2. **Create and broadly circulate a brochure-length synopsis of American evangelicalism,** its doctrinal-theological shortcomings in terms of outcomes (fruit), compared with classic Wesleyan theological principles which can produce better outcomes.

3. **Give priority commitment to publishing and producing "recital" oriented resources.** History is "story", and stories capture the imagination of young and old alike.

4. **Develop an "ordination-track" for "lay" leaders to increase historical theological literacy.** Since equal clergy-lay representation in governance is a value in our church, our commitment to develop "godly competent leaders" should not be limited to our clergy. There must be a concern for equal distribution of not only "voice and vote" but historical/theological competency.

5. **Greater "quality assurance" standards in the ordination process.** It is undeniable that we must exercise great flexibility in our ordination processes and requirements to fit the diverse life-situations of our emerging clergy. But our "flexing" should not result in a relaxing of standards of proficiency in theology, history and polity.

## CHAPTER 2
# Free Methodist Trajectories: The Road We Took

Stan Ingersol
Denominational Archivist, Church of the Nazarene

The Free Methodist Church has a soul. The question is: What is its character? Does the Free Methodist soul today reflect the deep impress of the church's founders? Or has the church, over time, developed a very different kind of soul?

Have Free Methodists, for instance, developed a *Baptist* soul over the years? Or perhaps an *American* soul? Has the church developed a *Republican* soul? Could the soul of Free Methodism today be described as the soul of "generic evangelicalism"? These questions need to be addressed.

### Free Methodism's Original Trajectory

Every denomination begins with a unique trajectory. At the beginning, that trajectory is set by the larger purpose and aims that give rise to the denomination.

For early Free Methodism, the larger purpose was to create a reformed Methodism. The specific aims can be identified as ...

> Early Free Methodists believed the gospel called them to establish urban churches that would welcome the poor and not permit distinctions based on wealth or literacy.

- A concern to preserve a form of Methodism that was centered, still, in the religion of the warmed heart.
- The desire for a more democratic Methodism.
- The conviction that the African slave deserved freedom, and after emancipation that newly freed men and women should be educated.
- The conviction that faithfulness to the gospel called Free Methodists to establish urban churches, especially

churches that would be welcoming to the poor and would not permit class distinctions based on wealth or literacy.
- A desire to participate in a true "believers' church" in the Wesleyan tradition.

Let's look at each trait briefly.

*The religion of the warmed heart.* The "religion of the warmed heart" stood at the center of early Methodist experience. Two things, particularly, marked the rise of Wesleyan Methodism in England. The first was the concern for a vital Christian experience. This was evident in
- the Wesleys' emphasis on a Christian faith that was personal,
- the importance they attached to the quest for Christian perfection or holiness,
- their commitment to the class meeting as the place where saints were held accountable for their progress in the faith.

The Methodist Episcopal Church had become America's largest denomination by the mid-19th century. It was also on pace to become the nation's most geographically diffused denomination — which it did in fact become. But rising middle-class prosperity among Methodists in the Eastern states facilitated change within their churches. Church choirs and professional singers began slowly replacing congregational song, making worship less participatory and more of a spectacle. The class meeting, once the basic unit of Methodism, was on the verge of no longer being mandatory and was about to experience a sharp decline. Congregations in larger cities became absorbed with building neo-Gothic edifices and fitting them with expensive church organs. And concern for the rising tide of urban poor was not nearly as evident in 19th-century American Methodism as it had been in British Methodism during Wesley's day.

So it was over against these changes that the Free Methodist dissent was raised. Strong evidence of the priority that B.T. Roberts gave to the warmed heart and the disciplined life was evident in the title of his paper, *The Earnest Christian*.

*A more democratic Methodism.* In the beginning Free Methodism adopted a structure that enshrined a democratic form of Methodism. It was not alone. A small series of new denominations were formed between 1830 and 1910, each as a different expression of democratic Methodism. Each one had its own reasons for not uniting with earlier ones, largely because their points of dissent were not identical. But all developed partly in relation to ongoing tensions over the nature and scope of episcopal authority in the Methodist Episcopal Church.

The Methodist Protestant Church (1830), the Wesleyan Methodist Connection (1843), and the Church of the Nazarene (1908) were among these new groups. Though each had a different vision of democratic Methodism, they shared the conviction that democratic processes and limits had to moderate episcopal authority. Methodist Protestants and Wesleyan Methodists did away with bishops altogether. Free Methodists and Nazarenes changed the office to "general superintendent," revised its powers, and located it within a democratic system far in advance of their common mother church.

The Free Methodist Church, like these others, retained the root conviction that guides all Methodist polity. This is the conviction that no specific design for church government is revealed in Holy Writ; therefore, the appropriate forms of church governance can be shaped by "common consent" as long as nothing agreed on violates the Word of God.

John Wesley himself came to this conviction late in life. In this equation, *mission* can shape *structure*. These assumptions gave British Methodism a structure *without* bishops and American Methodism (laboring in a different social and religious context) a structure *with* bishops. The essence of Methodist governance is not a particular type of episcopacy, nor episcopacy itself, but this assumption regarding church governance. The Free Methodist founders felt free to fashion a system that reflected their ideals and fit their mission.

B.T. Roberts' objection to lodge membership can be seen as part of this commitment to a democratic style of governance. He opposed the secret societies (especially the Masons and

Odd Fellows) because they bred a "brotherhood" mentality that was restrictive — a brotherhood not open to all but only to "the right kind" of people. Moreover, fraternal ties seemed to compete with the ordained ministry's own brotherhood ideal, dividing the ministers who should be united by their ordination vows into "insider" and "outsider" groups. Roberts also believed that certain ministers were stationed according to lodge ties, not a congregation's needs or a given minister's ability to meet them. Therefore an ideal at the heart of Methodism's appointive system was being defeated by an elitism based on an alternative brotherhood. He opposed it.

*The slave's freedom.* The slavery issue troubled the Methodist Episcopal Church from its beginning. An early stricture on slavery adopted by the founding Christmas Conference in 1784 was laid aside the following year by the church's southern conferences. In 1843, Wesleyan Methodists left because the M.E. Church had not condemned slavery and did not appear likely to do so. In 1844, the M.E. Church itself divided — one church for the North, another for the South. Even so the northern church's general conference refused to condemn slavery, fearing that annual conferences in the border states would unite with "the Church South" if they did so.

Opposition to slavery was critical in Free Methodism's rise. Abolitionist sentiments, heightened by perfectionist tendencies, fired the hearts of Free Methodists in 1860.

*A heart for the poor.* Not only vital Christian experience but also concern for the poor marked the rise of British Methodism. Had the Wesleys not taken their ministry to the condemned prisoners awaiting execution, to London's poor, to dockhands in Bristol and miners at Kingswood, and to many similar places, the Methodist chapter in Christian history would be just a few sentences, a mere footnote about English religious societies of the 18th century. Instead it can truly be said that wherever the poor gathered, so did the Methodists. This is what caused Methodism to burn with a strong, bright flame during the lifetime of the Wesleys.

A century later, that was no longer true. In America, fashionable Methodist churches in the East rented pews to their wealthier members to help retire church debts. Those who could not afford a rented pew sat in less desirable parts of the sanctuary. Roberts objected that rich and poor were treated differently, and this was neither true Christianity nor true Methodism. In contrast, the Free Methodist *Discipline* required that all pews be free. Early Free Methodists deliberately planted churches among the poor.

*A believers' church.* The believers' church aspect of early Free Methodism (that is, the church restricted to genuine sincere believers) was implicit, rather than explicit, but nevertheless quite real. Believers' churches arise when a body of Christians believe their mother church has become lax in its disciplinary standards. This laxity, in their view, threatens the church's integrity. They want a church that is holy, that seeks to maintain ecclesiastical holiness by applying discipline where severe offenses occur. Believers' churches are marked by zeal, which they view as a contrast to the easy and comfortable Christianity of larger and less disciplined churches. Clearly Free Methodism functioned as a believers' church over against the much larger Methodist mother church that the founders believed was compromised.

We who belong to believers' churches in the Wesleyan tradition generally give little thought, however, to our underlying ecclesiology. This omission is critical, because without attention to how we understand "church" we can drift to places where we would not choose to go if we were conscious of it.

I believe that there is a high road and a low road within the believers' church tradition.

The low road is illustrated by the Baptist churches where "soul liberty" is highly prized. This type of believers' church is rooted in radical individualism. The church is essentially an association of individuals.

The high road in the believers' church tradition places far more importance on the corporate or communal nature of the church. It sees the church as the place where a holy people is made. Mennonites and Church of the Brethren are good examples of believers' churches that have taken this higher road.

Believers' churches on the low road more obviously reflect

American democratic assumptions, such as decisions by majority vote. Churches that take the high road are more inclined to work on an issue until they find consensus, for they take the fellowship quite seriously.

Which road have Free Methodists taken? And what difference could it make if more careful reflection were encouraged here?

**Radical Wesleyanism in Context**

We have looked at five specific aims of the first Free Methodists. The first aim can be seen as a desire to preserve the spiritual traditions of Methodism. It is thus conservative in its thrust and implications.

The four other aims, however, were all radical in their basic impulse. So they justify speaking of Free Methodism as an expression of radical Wesleyanism. In certain respects, early Free Methodism had strong affinities with the radical holiness of other contemporary movements, including Charles G. Finney and the Oberlin tradition, and the Wesleyan Methodist Connection that preceded Free Methodism by nearly two decades.

To appreciate the uniqueness of radical Wesleyanism, let's compare it to a more socially conservative expression of the Wesleyan-holiness vision.

I assume your general knowledge of the basic outline of B.T. Roberts' life and work. As a pastor in New York State, he engaged in a controversy with what he called "New School Methodism." He supported the abolition of slavery and regarded the general conference of the Methodist Episcopal Church as morally tepid for its equivocation on ending slavery, especially after the Southern conferences created a separate denomination. He opposed the elitism of secret societies. And he wanted churches that treated the poor with respect, rather than churches that reinforced distinctions based on wealth or class.

Some of Roberts' concerns were not really shared by many early Free Methodists. He firmly supported women's right to preach, to be ordained for Christian ministry, and to exercise pastoral authority within the church. He tried more than once to convince the Free Methodist general conference to see the issue his way but failed. His church moved toward his position only well after his death. His advocacy on this issue places him in the select company of people like Jarena Lee (African Methodist Episcopal), Catherine Booth (Salvation Army), Luther Lee (Wesleyan Methodist), Lee Anna Starr (Methodist Protestant), Fannie McDowell Hunter (Nazarene) and one of his own successors, Bishop Walter Sellew.

Consider a contemporary of Roberts who agreed with him on many things but devoted his life to constructing a very different type of Methodist church. His name was Lovick Pierce. Like Roberts, Pierce believed that primitive Methodism's rich patrimony was being squandered by sophisticated but theologically careless churchmen. He embraced the *Way of Holiness*, the first holiness journal published in the South. In it he described his attempts over a lifetime to promote entire sanctification at Methodist camp meetings. The failure of the doctrine to impress the church, he wrote, was because the church contained thousands of denominational but unconverted Methodists. ... [W]henever we appoint a sanctification prayer meeting, or seek to form an association for the promotion of holiness and appeal to this class, it is shocking to see the prevarications of these unspiritually minded professors when we feel moved to call on the church to move in these lines of consecration to God, and of a wider, deeper work of grace in the heart. ... [I]t is useless to preach sanctification to a church membership living so far below this plane of religion as not to feel its necessity.[1]

Some twenty years later, Pierce's *Miscellaneous Essay on Entire Sanctification* reiterated these themes of spiritual laxity, the lowering of membership standards, and the decline of interest in godliness and the sanctified life among Methodists.[2]

Such words and sentiments could have been written by B.T. Roberts or John Wesley Redfield. Instead they were written by a Wesleyan-holiness preacher who helped construct a Methodist denomination around the proposition that slavery should be defended by law and argument and maintained by force of arms if necessary. Pierce entered the ministry of the Georgia Conference in 1804 and was a delegate to every General Conference between 1824 and 1844. When Methodism divided over slavery, he helped organize the Methodist Episcopal Church, South. He was sent north to the northern body's General Conference in 1848, but once there the northern Methodists refused to recognize the fraternal delegates from the South — a public repudiation that came to symbolize the deep alienation between the northern and southern branches of Episcopal Methodism. Pierce became an elder statesman and held "a unique position of leadership in the Church, South" as "a guiding influence in its affairs."[3] He preached at the consecration services of various bishops and in 1854 witnessed his son's election as bishop. In his last years, he was the "grand old man" of Southern Methodism.

Pierce became very unlike Madison, Jefferson, Washington, and other Southern founders of the American Republic, who affirmed their belief in human equality despite the contradictions between that conviction and their own practice. Instead, Pierce eventually bought into a doctrine of human inequality propagated by states' rights theorists and pro-slavery ideologues such as John C. Calhoun. And that belief in human inequality, designed to bolster the ideological defense of slavery, reinforced the conviction that a hierarchically-structured society was God-ordained and sustained by divine will. In such a social order, the rights of women and African Americans were held hostage.

The propositions to which Lovick Pierce dedicated his life could not provide a more striking contrast to the radical Wesleyanism of B.T. Roberts.

A half-century ago, Timothy Smith argued that revivalism releases creative new energies that can alter society. In *Revivalism and Social Reform*, Smith built his case from abundant evidence, appraising revivalism as a positive social force. Smith's intent was to counter the persistent stereotype of his day that revivalism functions in socially conservative ways and helps maintain the status quo. Some of Smith's readers — primarily those who personally embrace the radical holiness tradition — tend to forget revivalism's socially conservative side. But revivalism in the ante-bellum South played a remarkably different social role in that context than it did in the examples that Smith used. This is illustrated by Lovick Pierce's story, documented thoroughly by historian Donald Matthews' book *Religion in the Old South*, and by the growing literature on Southern religion that has appeared in the past quarter-century.

Abolitionism is part of the heritage of the Wesleyan-holiness tradition, but so, too, is racism, slavery, segregation, and white flight to the suburbs. By the same token, concern for the poor is a part of our heritage, but so, too, is middle-class comfort and neglect of the poor.

We should be clear-eyed about our history and equally clear-eyed about what parts of it we intend to affirm and what parts we intend to overcome. And if we can no longer assert confidently that the holiness movement is a reliable friend of social progress, then what are we to make of Roberts' alliance of sanctification and social change? Should we not value it that much more highly?

## The Trajectory Altered

What forces exert change on the trajectory of a church in the Wesleyan-holiness tradition? Or to put it differently, what muddies our birthright?

***Heritage and Tradition.*** A heritage is essentially a legacy; what we inherit from the past. And what we inherit is often a mixture of both good and bad. If you inherit property or a business, for instance, you will also inherit any debt attached to it. A heritage can easily become muddied.

Tradition, though, is what we make of the heritage. The tradition is that part of the heritage where we choose to find our vision — the part we consciously choose to hold onto and live out of.

Here is an example. The Southern Baptist Convention was created solely to be a Baptist denomination in the South in which no one's honor would be impugned for owning and selling slaves. It came into existence for no other reason than the slavery issue. After the Civil War, the Southern Baptists lent their support to the Jim Crow laws that disenfranchised and socially segregated hundreds of thousands of black Freedmen. Collusion with slavery and segregation was both the Southern

Baptist heritage and tradition and remained so over 150 years.

Several years ago, however, the Southern Baptists began publicly repenting for their past behavior. They made acts of contrition in special ceremonies of confession and repentance, and did so in the presence of Black Baptists. Denominations can rarely escape the thrust of their founders' vision, but the Southern Baptists have taken steps to change, to start new tradition, to replace bad tradition with good tradition.

Every denomination accumulates accretions that become part of the heritage. Whether or not these accretions remain part of the tradition, however, can be a matter of conscious choice. What accretions has Free Methodism accumulated?

***The Distortions of Fundamentalism.*** The conflict between fundamentalists and modernists developed in the early 20th century and sharpened in the 1920s. Free Methodist sympathies were clearly on fundamentalism's side and against religious skepticism, the higher critics of the Bible, the Darwinists, and the liberal Protestant theologies. And in its opposition to theological modernism, the Free Methodist Church underwent a fundamentalist phase, as did other evangelical and Wesleyan churches.

Every evangelical denomination faced a critical question as the conflict between fundamentalism and modernism grew sharper. How extensively would fundamentalism alter the church's self-understanding? Free Methodism originated with a distinct identity. Would that identity persist as the fundamentalist crusade developed? Or would it be lost, swallowed up by a growing affinity with a newer widespread 20$^{th}$-century movement whose spirit and purposes were quite different from those of the radical Wesleyans who birthed Free Methodist identity in the first place?

The issue is drawn even more clearly when we consider the nature of movements. All movements share certain features, whether they are religious or social in nature. Movements are not bred by consensus; they are born of dissent.

Lawrence Goodwyn's history of the populist movement of the late 19th century is a helpful place to start for understanding movements. In *The Populist Moment,* Goodwyn argues that a new movement begins because people analyze a particular set of conditions. That analysis must seem convincing, at least to some of the people affected. Spokesmen who believe the analysis must be recruited, or else the analysis goes nowhere. The spokesmen spread the ideas of the movement and recruit new believers. Since the establishment controls the press, a movement must generate its own publishing enterprise. Tracts, booklets, broadsheets and periodicals produced by the movement assist in recruitment and help the movement consolidate its gains. Meetings and conventions rally the faithful and energize them. Goodwyn stresses the vital significance of a movement maintaining its focus. His thesis, highly provocative, is that populism began as an agrarian revolt that achieved nearly all the basic steps but failed to mature as a political movement when populists began sharing their platforms with the advocates of the free silver campaign. This muddied the agrarian message, altered populism's objectives, and led to the movement's rapid demise.[4]

Free Methodism began with its own analysis of the state of American religion, particularly within the Methodist Episcopal Church. Free Methodist leaders diagnosed the problem within Methodism as declension, or decline, as they witnessed the erosion of loyalties to the class meeting and other mechanisms designed to foster Christian holiness. They viewed the problem of Methodism as a compromise with the spirit of this world, expressed in different ways — uncritical acceptance of Freemasonry, temporizing on the issue of slavery, and a willingness to distinguish between different classes of people based on their income or lack of one.

They responded by creating a reform movement. They offered spiritual and practical solutions to the growing spiritual laxity and doctrinal confusion over the theology and social application of Christian holiness. Their critique of creeping formalism and a religious culture compromised by growing middle-class prosperity was developed long before Darwin and the higher critics of the Bible had any discernible impact on American Protestant churches at large. Free Methodism used evangelists as spokesmen, and developed a press that was independent of the Methodist bishops. As Free Methodism emerged as a separate denomination, it viewed itself as faithful to the ideals of Wesley and historic Methodism.

Fundamentalism however (arising several decades later) analyzed the religious problem much differently. And so they generated a different set of answers and developed a different agenda. The fundamentalists analyzed the problem at the heart of American religion as "liberalism," as underscored in J. Gresham Machen's classic battle text, *Christianity and Liberalism* (1923). Machen represented the historic Princeton school of theology, a conservative strain of Presbyterian thought that regarded Wesleyan theology as a dangerous Pelagian highway, a conservative precursor of the liberal problem. The evangelists who served as fundamentalism's primary spokesmen, and the fundamentalist press at large, were indifferent to the primary concerns of radical Wesleyanism and antagonistic, for the most part, to Methodist theology.

To be sure, there are places where the complaints of Free Methodism's founders and the fundamentalists appeared to intersect. For instance, many fundamentalists, committed to dispensational premillennialism, judged the large popular denominations to be apostate and fallen. This could be linked to B.T. Roberts' complaint that the established churches were formal and cold. The complaints appear similar but are not the same.

The primary challenge a denomination faces when intersected by another influential movement is this: The leaders of the new movement have their own agenda, rooted in their own dissent. As they encounter existing organizations, they seek implicitly (and sometimes explicitly) to supplant a Christian organization's founding vision with a different vision — namely, their own.

How deeply did fundamentalism threaten the unique identify of Free Methodists? And how did Free Methodists respond?

***The Magnetic Pull of the Evangelical Mainstream.*** As the Free Methodist Church aged, it edged increasingly toward the mainstream of American evangelicalism. Fundamentalism provided an important push, but it was hardly the only force at work.

That evangelical mainstream is a work-in-progress even today. It is undergoing continual development. Never static, it always changes. Methodism played a key role in shaping the evangelical mainstream of the 19th century. Methodists owned an exceedingly small share of the American religious franchise in 1775. By 1850, however, Methodism's two branches, north and south, constituted the largest religious block in the nation. Other American churches were strongly influenced by Methodist ways.

But this changed in the 20th century. By 1920, the Methodist Episcopal Church was marked by so much theological pluralism that it was no longer regarded as a reliable evangelical ally. Moreover, a sudden surge of Baptist energies pushed Baptists well ahead of Methodists by mid-century. Then came the growth of Pentecostal and charismatic denominations later in the 20th century. So we can think of the 19th century as the Methodist century, and the 20th century as the Baptist and Pentecostal century. We can only imagine what the 21st century will be.

> As the Free Methodist Church aged, it edged increasingly toward the mainstream of American evangelicalism.

American evangelicalism is in motion, but it is not a movement in the same sense that fundamentalism was — except in its desire to shed the narrow-mindedness and undesirable image of fundamentalism. Evangelicalism is not rooted in dissent, as genuine movements are, but reflects the more theologically conservative instincts of those churches and individuals which face modernity but are generally uncomfortable with hard-line fundamentalism on the right and the ecumenical movement on the left. Instead, evangelicals find a sense of connection with one another across theological boundaries based on their shared commitment to various forms of orthodox Protestantism.

We might think of today's popular evangelicalism as the water in which we swim.

Churches gravitate toward the evangelical mainstream for

various reasons. Often they want to conform. Their wild and wooly days are over and they want to be respectable. They also gravitate toward evangelicalism because they may fail at their catechetical tasks. The people — Wesleyan people — sometimes can no longer distinguish between the Wesleyan message and the message of radio and television preachers. There is tremendous pressure to polish away the rough edges of the Wesleyan vision and yield to a generic evangelicalism.

Several years ago the renowned historian Martin Marty wrote a perceptive article on the corrosive influence of generic evangelicalism. It was titled "Baptistification Takes Over." Marty is a Lutheran, and his primary point was to lament the way in which very un-Lutheran ideas, drawn largely from popular evangelicalism, are reshaping liturgical churches.[5] But his concern should also resonate with us. Popular notions of baptism, popular eschatology, and the worship wars are only a few of the areas where the water in which we swim is affecting the life of Wesleyan churches and reshaping our theology and practice.

This doesn't mean we shouldn't learn from other traditions. We should. But it means that we need to be deliberate, take steps and undertake the serious work needed to understand what it means for Free Methodists and other Wesleyans to function as believers' churches in the Wesleyan tradition.

*The influence of American culture.* You do not really need a historian's perspective on this one, so I'll make two brief points.

First, if the evangelical subculture is the water in which we swim, American culture is the air we breathe. We are constantly taking it in and out.

Second, being children of our culture is very much a mixed bag.

On one hand our culture bombards us with messages that

clearly shape our identities as individuals and churches. Some messages tell us that we are primarily sexual beings who will find happiness dressing a certain way, applying certain brands of make-up, and frequenting certain entertainments. Other messages urge us to consume, convincing us that happiness comes through owning a certain type of house, living in a certain neighborhood, driving a certain car, having a computer or entertainment center with the latest gizmos, staying up with the Joneses. Other messages claim that a test of true faith comes through voting for the candidates of a certain political party, or supporting certain social issues, or exhibiting a certain type of patriotism.

And yet, not all assumptions drawn from our culture are bad. American political culture inspired Free Methodism's early commitment to a more democratic and participatory style of Methodism, and this was a good thing. Indeed, I believe the Holy Spirit's voice is heard far more readily in churches where the Spirit is allowed to speak through the whole people of God than in hierarchical churches where senior administrators claim to discern God's will and interpret it for the people.

So we are called to sift the influence of our culture, just as we are called to sift our place in the evangelical world, and just as we are called to sift our own heritage.

Just over a decade ago, Martin Marty was the keynote speaker at a conference of Nazarene sociologists of religion. The theme of "the elusive Nazarene identity" ran like a thread through several presentations that year. At the end of the conference, Marty was asked to comment.

Marty noted that he had listened to discussions about the Willow Creek church as a model for ministry, a perceived loss of Nazarene identity, and other subjects. His opinion, though, was that if Nazarenes wanted to learn from the Willow Creek model, they should study Willow Creek theology, since theological assumptions always underlie a particular method. He warned, though, that this approach would facilitate, not deter, a sense of drift within the denomination. Rather than aping the models around us, he urged us to go back and study the lives and intentions of our founders, then undertake the difficult task of asking how those intentions can be applied in our day.

It was good advice, though the Nazarenes have rarely followed it since it was given. May you Free Methodists do better.

## Endnotes

1. *Way of Holiness* (May 1876): 18-21; quote from p. 20; also see the article by Pierce entitled "The experience and observations of Rev. L. Pierce on sanctification for seventy one years," ibid., (April 1876): 13-16.
2. Lovick Pierce, A *Miscellaneous Essay on Entire Sanctification: showing How it was Lost from the Church, and How it May and Must be Regained* (Nashville: Publishing House of the M. E. Church, South, 1897).
3. James P. Pilkington, "Lovick Pierce," in *The Encyclopedia of World Methodism* (Nashville: Parthenon Press for the United Methodist Publishing House, 1974) 2:1909.
4. Lawrence Goodwyn, *The Populist Moment: A Short History of the Agrarian Revolt in America* (Oxford, London, and New York: Oxford University Press, 1978). *The Populist Moment* is an abridgement of a more comprehensive work, *Democratic Promise: The Populist Movement in America* (1976).
5. Martin E. Marty, "Baptistification Takes Over," *Christianity Today* (September 2, 1983): 33-36.

## CHAPTER 3
# Growing Up Free Methodist

Linda Adams
Pastor, New Hope Free Methodist Church
Rochester, New York

In his chapter, Doug Newton reminded us of the need to recite our history to one another and gave us a glimpse into his own personal history in the Free Methodist Church. I begin with some personal reflections, as well.

I am a daughter of the Free Methodist Church. And I guess you could say, if the church has grandchildren, I'm one of those, too. The Most Holy Faith was passed on to me not through my grandmother Lois and my mother Eunice, but through my grandmothers Lola and Fern, and my mother Estella. And, apparently unlike Timothy, I was privileged to be guided and influenced also by my father Ken and my grandfathers Vernon and Robert, all of them Free Methodists — Grandpa Cleveland being a pastor in the East Michigan Conference.

The Cleveland grandparents' influence was mostly indirect, since they both died when I was fairly young. But Grandma Cleveland's funeral is my earliest vivid memory of a worship service. I will never forget the singing or that strange, undeniable mixture of grief and joy. (By the way, the song "Until Then" was introduced as a favorite song of hers, and I just figured out about a month ago that it was basically a contemporary song when she loved it! It was written in 1951 and she went home to be with the Lord about 1963.)

Both the Beardslee and the Cleveland clans have stayed close over the years, and we've created some opportunities for the kind of "recitals" Doug Newton writes about. For instance, both sides of the family have organized reunions for several days at a stretch, and included interviews with my parents' generation, which were videotaped for posterity, and family trivia games that my cousin and sister created to counteract the curvature of memory. Oh, yes, and the thousands of Aunt Thelma's slides ... !

My most personal insights into Grandpa Cleveland came when my mom transcribed his diaries from the war years and distributed them to us all a few years ago. Besides the many descriptions of worship services, prayer meetings, and visiting musicians, there was the delightful, recurring sentence, "After dinner Mother and I walked over town for an ice cream." Ahh, *now* they're a real couple! It also takes the edge off some of the stories of poverty that I've heard. They could afford meat only once a year, but they found a way to get ice cream. (I guess I come by that vice naturally.)

One more memory needs to be indulged, since we are considering Free Methodism's historic identity. My family attended the East Michigan Family Camp only on Sundays, since our home conference was Southern Michigan (where we went for the whole camp). Every year we got to East Michigan Camp for the final Sunday, in time to hear Eileen Bovee sing "The Holy City."

I don't remember any of the colorful emotional displays Doug Newton talks about in his chapter, but maybe there are some generational and regional differences at work here. Perhaps the Michigan camp meetings cooled off earlier than those in western New York.

Speaking of cooling off, I remember sweltering in the tabernacle, then returning to the Cleveland tent to drink from the common metal dipper that hung by the water bucket outside Grandma's tent. I knew about germs by then, so my drinking from the Cleveland dipper was a conscious choice to catch whatever my family had. Thankfully, I caught more than whatever the dipper passed on.

The church of my childhood was very different from the one Doug describes. I grew up in the college town of Spring Arbor, Michigan, on Planet Big Church. Once a month we children were dismissed from the Sunday morning service to go to JMS (Junior Missionary Society) where two ancient ladies,

Mrs. Heltzel and Miss Edna Lohr, captivated us with flannelgraphs and tales of foreign missions. I don't remember which one of them told the story the day I memorized Isaiah 53:6 and gave my heart to Jesus, but the visual image of that flannel lamb straying from the fold and "the Lord laying on Jesus the iniquity of us all" is in my head for life! Mel Gibson's *The Passion of the Christ* quoted from the same chapter and gave me some multi-million dollar new images, but they haven't replaced that early formative one.

Church was pretty "safe and comfortable" until my teen years. Then, thank God, the Asbury Revival of 1970 broke out and spilled over to us. When the Holy Spirit moved in a mighty way over the next months and even years, all the ordinary ways of doing church went out the window. We were literally at the church building seven days a week for many, many months. Our high school youth group went from sitting in the balcony — chewing gum, passing notes and flirting with each other — to front and center, right down in the middle of the Glory Circle. We knelt at the altar for hours, weeping and repenting and worshipping. We laid hands on people and they were healed! We sang and testified and watched the Holy Spirit fall on people in convicting power, prompting instantaneous confession, reconciliation, and restitution. We took on the local high school, gathering for prayer before we got on the buses in the morning, pasting so many Jesus stickers all over the building that they had to make a rule against them! We proclaimed, "Once you've tasted the sweet wine of Jesus, everything else is just Kool-Aid!" (Ironic metaphor, coming from a bunch of teetotaling teenagers!)

We also found out that the passions of revival can bring in their wake controversy and secret meetings that end up in church splits. When our beloved pastor mysteriously left to start a non-denominational church just up the road, amid accusations of tongues-speaking and fanaticism, I pleaded with my parents, "Why don't we go with them?" My dad's answer was simple — maybe oversimplified. "We are Free Methodists." That explanation never set too well with me.

A sweet footnote from a few years later: That new church nurtured my future husband in the faith when he came to

Christ at the age twenty-six, so our marriage reunited the two congregations for a day!

## The Call to Ministry

It was in the Spring Arbor church in 1972 that I received my call into ministry. Retired missionary Alice Taylor preached and dozens of young people, mostly college students, streamed down the aisles to respond to God's call to ministry. I didn't know what that call would look like — I never dreamed I'd be a pastor, having never seen a female pastor, but I "signed a blank check" and gave my life to God for whatever he wanted of it.

How on earth did a commitment to urban ministry emerge from a background like mine? That's where the story takes some geographical twists and turns, too long to relate here. But that's also where the Usable History of the Free Methodist Church consciously kicked in.

FM church planter Dwight Gregory came to Spring Arbor College with a hokey little hand-written flyer that said, "Go East, Young Man (or Woman)!" John and I took him up on it. He was planting a church in Passaic, New Jersey, across from New York City, and needed some free co-laborers.

Well, we didn't do it for free; they paid us $12.50 a week. But Dwight, Howard Olver, Howard Snyder, Donna Saylor and all those people meeting annually at CUE (Continental Urban Exchange) were in the process of recovering the passion of the founders. They saw huge urban populations with minimal access to the gospel, and they were going to make a dent. They had a goal worth sacrificing for — actually a dual goal, with a familiar ring — to spread the message of biblical Christianity in the cities, and to preach the gospel to the poor.

For at least a dozen years, CUE became John's and my primary "conference." More than any other place in the denomination at the time, CUE represented for us passionate worship, intercessory prayer, and a welcoming of people who didn't fit the then-dominant Free Methodist mold — African Americans, Hispanics — and, as I was coming to find out, people like *me*, in that oxymoronic "women pastors" category. I was searching for the Free Methodist soul, and I found it at CUE.

## Locating the Free Methodist Soul

This leads to the main question here: Engaging the Free Methodist soul. Preparing to speak at the first (2004) "Search for the Free Methodist Soul" symposium in Indianapolis, I sent an email to a few friends, asking for their input. Here's what I wrote:

> The symposium is a cross-generational dialogue on what is the essence of Free Methodism. Is there any core of who we are that needs to be preserved from the "melting pot" of "generic evangelicalism"? What is that? What is our soul, our key identity, our unique charism that we are charged by God to live out, and to bring to the larger Body of Christ and to the world? Are we truly meant to be "just Christians" or is there something important also about being Free Methodists?
>
> I know there's some feeling that we keep casting about for the latest solution or paradigm that will help us reach the lost, accomplish our mission, grow, etc. Yet over the decades it starts to feel like a loss of soul while we chase fads and methodologies. We change structures, we drop unhelpful denominational quirks or legalistic traditions, but what should we hold on to?

Once I started thinking about this, I began to notice this same quest all over the map among American churches. *Christianity Today* reported that the Southern Baptists were trying to change their name. They are no longer primarily a Southern U.S. denomination; they have churches all over the world. So their name is misleading and unhelpful. But to disconnect "Southern" from "Baptist" would be to lop off one of the golden arches! It's their logo, their tag, their identity. It's not going to be an easy transition, I predict.

> Who's to say which of our distinctives need to be outgrown and which need to be preserved at all costs?

I also read about Max Lucado and his local congregation's "morphing" the church of Christ. He and several others had publicly repudiated their cardinal doctrine of baptismal regeneration, and his church added instrumental music to two of the three worship services. Probably most of us would applaud those changes, at least the doctrinal one, and say it's a good thing to outgrow your denomination's limiting distinctives if they're *wrong!* But who's to say which of our distinctives need to be outgrown and which need to be preserved at all costs? That's the sifting that Stan Ingersol encourages us to do in his chapter, "Free Methodist Trajectories." The challenge is to shape the tradition by how we choose to receive and pass on the heritage, with its mixed bag of strengths and weaknesses.

When I sent my email about this symposium, and also when I sat down for coffee with several pastors, I got a lot of different perspectives. One was defensive: "Who says we've lost our soul?" (I told him I didn't think anyone was accusing us of that, but that it doesn't hurt any person or group to take inventory every once in a while.) As individuals, we *are* a soul; we *have* a body. We take our bodies in for an annual physical. Since the soul is less tangible, we might decide we need to haul it in for an occasional diagnostic once-over. The same goes for a denomination. I am not insulted by the question.

Another interpreted the question as, "When are we at our best?" — and answered, "When we give people a second chance. We believe in restorative grace, so when pastors or other people fail, we have a process to help them move toward wholeness. Our process orientation toward grace gives people the opportunity to move on with God from any place on the continuum." That is a rather unique way to define our identity, but I think it identifies the characteristic that most people at my local church would lift up, the undeniable mark of New Hope Free Methodist Church.

Another pastor asked, "Do we have to distinguish our soul's characteristics from other holiness or Wesleyan groups? Isn't our best self their best self? We all want to follow John Wesley in defining the *summum bonum* as 'perfect love.'" I responded, just because my family sits down to talk about how to be the best nuclear family we can be, that doesn't mean we have to define family differently from or similarly to my sister and her family. Maybe we would come up with exactly the same concerns and constellation of traits, but I doubt it.

Take a look at the "sort of" Free Methodist Quadrilateral in chapter 10 of this book. It pictures Free Methodism as drawing together (or perhaps being pulled apart by) four tendencies: "Anglo-Catholic," "Evangelical," "Charismatic," and "Anabaptist." Where do most of us, and our churches, fit?

If we're being balanced and looking to synthesize, it's hard to pin it down or pigeonhole our identity. All four of these tendencies are a part of our history and our current identity, though in differing degrees. For instance, we cherish the sacraments and value tradition, in common with the Anglo-Catholic part of our heritage. The Evangelical strain highlights the need for personal conversion, the commitment to the authority of the Scriptures, and a mission-driven pull toward reaching the lost, often expressed in church-growth efforts and a yearning for revival.

But that's not all of who we are. We also have strong roots, through our founders, in social holiness, social justice, a concern for preaching the gospel to the poor and obeying the ethical demands of the Scriptures. These we share with the Anabaptist tradition (such as Mennonites and many Brethren groups). And yet we are more than that. In common with charismatic Christians, we emphasize the role of the Holy Spirit in giving gifts and making holiness possible. We own a heritage that holds firmly to the possibilities of love that sanctification brings.

We believe a *biblical synthesis* holds these all in creative tension. How much easier it might be to just "land in a corner"! But we want to be and do more than that. Our "soul" lives in the intersecting middle. At its best, Free Methodism is sacramental, evangelical, radically obedient, and Spirit-filled.

One person I talked with about Free Methodist identity rephrased the question this way: What is our unique charism, or spiritual gift? What special gift has God given us that he wants us to share? This person's answer was *holiness* — real, experiential, Holy Spirit filled, disciplined, but not legalistic or judgmental, holy love. That key doctrine, wed to vital practice, must remain alive in groups of people — and that is our high calling and privilege.

**New Paradigms? A New Identity?**

In my adult lifetime I have seen Free Methodists embrace several new paradigms or methodologies to help us "get the job done." Each of these has had its day: Church growth seminars, Growing a Healthy Church, Small Groups as The Paradigm, Contemporary Music, CEO Leadership Model, Seeker-Sensitive Approach, Purpose-Driven churches. We have not always been careful about the presuppositions and theological underpinnings of these movements. One pastor told me, "We're pragmatists. We use whatever works. That's the way to get missional." Is this really what we're about?

> "We're pragmatists. We use whatever works. That's the way to get missional," one pastor said.

But several of the pastors I consulted felt that as a denomination we have gradually changed our expectations of pastors. The push is toward "success," however defined. We pastors go to various conference and regional gatherings, hungry for some soul food. But often we get fed the latest, greatest way to get more productive. We leave wearied by the sinking feeling that we've yet again observed a "successful thing" that we can't duplicate. One pastor went so far as to say, "We've prostituted ourselves on the altar of productive ministry."

Well, here is my own confession. I am a graduate of the Beeson Doctor of Ministry program at Asbury Seminary. I saw many wonderful things, and I learned a lot — some of which I've had to unlearn. I also resisted things I recognized as being very out of touch with Free Methodist (and biblical) sensibilities regarding the poor and marginalized and other basic Wesleyan themes.

But then in Korea I heard the pastor of the Kwang Lim

Methodist Church in Seoul tell us that he prays three to four hours every morning. This in addition to the all-night vigils, regular fasts, and other prayer times. And I read that Pastor Paul Yonggi Cho says the same thing about the Yoiddo Full Gospel Church's phenomenal growth. The secret is prayer. Prayer mountains, prayer retreats, daily pre-dawn prayer sessions the whole church attends.

Like other visiting American pastors, I was impressed with these Christians' devotion — but then at home I tried to copy their strategic organizing rather than their strategic prayer! If one paragraph of their book tells of their prayer life and one hundred pages tell about organizing cell groups and growing a church of hundreds of thousands, my American self will jump to the "doable" part and miss the whole point.

Every pastor I know has shelf after shelf of expensive notebooks, filled with one program after another, each guaranteed to revolutionize our ministry or grow our church. But with very little to show for it.

A key issue here is ministerial identity. Eugene Peterson's books sound the cry over and over again: We can too easily lose our souls by "running a church." The demands of the job description are not right. If we simply fulfill our people's expectations, or even our superintendents' expectations, we can easily lose our souls along the way. Busyness and "running a church" cannot be the *heart* of our ministry, yet we fall prey to that pressure. Peterson points out that he and his wife "run a house" — yes, they take out garbage and pay bills and paint the porch — but their life together is not about "running a house"! They are nurturing and sustaining and celebrating a Christian marriage and home — a cameo of Christ and the church. Running the house is just the functional necessity.

We pastors often get caught inside our own heads, seeing ourselves as "church-runners" rather than shepherds. The "cure of souls" is no longer our priority, and even our own souls get neglected in the process. Do we keep a Sabbath? Do we immerse ourselves in the Word of God?

What would it profit a denomination if we were to gain the

whole world, but lose our own soul? And what would we give in exchange for our soul?

If these issues of ministerial identity are true of pastors, do they also affect conference superintendents? Our conference websites mainly show forms and calendars and statistics. You may have to click several times before you see evidence of what we're really supposed to be most passionate about! And what of our understanding of the identity and role of bishops?

**The "Free" in Free Methodist**

So what does it mean today to be "Free" Methodists? How do we translate our original impulses for freedom (free pews, freedom for slaves, freedom from sin's bondage, freedom of the Spirit in worship) in today's world? Is "Free" supposed to mean new things in the New Day?

A key early Free Methodist commitment was freedom of the Spirit in worship. Some months ago several people from my church joined a community worship event at a Wesleyan Church. I was sitting with eight-year-old Monica. A man from Family Life Radio got up and preached, and his style was "old fashioned." When he built up a good head of steam, he got loud! Three times, when he was speaking so loudly that she couldn't be heard, Monica yelled into my ear, "That guy can really preach!!" The third time, he stopped "really preaching" right before her last two words, so everyone in our section turned around and smiled at us.

But I wondered, is Monica missing something at our church? By her definition, apparently, she'd never heard any "real preaching" from me. I talk with people. Beyond issues of style, have I lost something in passion? If I really believe what I'm saying, maybe it needs to come across more forcefully. Have I been seduced by a "seeker sensitivity" that has made me avoid intensity for the sake of not "weirding out" the visitors? More soul-searching.

I have spent a few years of my life worshipping in churches that are not Free Methodist. The thing that brought me back home was our position on women in ministry. This too is a key Free Methodist freedom. It is one of the things that cannot melt into the evangelical pot! Our founder, B.T. Roberts, valued that freedom and spent a lot of leadership capital fighting for it. Today, do we teach it, model it, and faithfully pass the baton to the next generation? Is equality in the New Community something people can feel when they come to our churches? It is in mine — but I fear that isn't always the case.

This discussion raises more questions than it answers. But we need these questions in order to stimulate good thinking and honest dialogue about our "heart and soul." My prayer is that Free Methodists will live out the very best of biblical Christianity, and that as we do so, this will fulfill the vision of our forebears — and, most importantly, the vision and calling of the Lord of the church. Let us pray and strive together to live from the center of who we are, faithfully embodying the soul of Free Methodism in the new millennium.

## CHAPTER 4
# *Embodying Our Mission*

Mark Van Valin
Pastor, Free Methodist Church
Spring Arbor, Michigan

For anyone to attempt to describe, let alone prescribe, the "soul" of Free Methodism is a bit presumptuous. I am just one pastor who, like many others, spends his days staying ahead of the calendar and the constant flow of human need. I can relate to the story of the man on the airplane who responded to the inquiring woman sitting next to him, "No, I am not a minister, I've just been sick for a few days." The best I can do is to share out of my own laboratory of ministry and comment anecdotally on what I have observed.

I am, as Donald Joy would say, a "blown in the bottle" Free Methodist. On the Van Valin side, my Free Methodist roots go back four generations before me. On the Imhoff side, they go back two. The network of friends and family across the church continues to be a great source of strength and blessing to me. I am indebted to the church. For me, it has always been loving, affirming, and gracious, seasoned with the smell of potluck macaroni and cheese.

The Free Methodist church that nurtured me was a mostly homogenous, ethnocentric culture. Every Sunday, from California to New York, everyone sang out of *Hymns of the Living Faith*. All my friends vacationed at the campground. The majority of the leaders I knew graduated from Greenville, and intermarriage was the only dance allowed. It was cause for celebration but you had to watch your step.

I have pastored full-time since 1983. I have lived in every holy city in the Midwest. I have served the church at a number of levels. Much like my own discovery of Jesus, I am still working my way out of the paper bag of my youth to re-covenant with my church in maturing love and loyalty.

With that background, I share with you several key convictions about the soul of Free Methodism.

## The FM "Soul" Found in our Original Mission

Over the last two decades, many of our churches have expended great energy and resources in writing and rewriting mission and purpose statements. I do not believe however that we can improve much on the earliest denominational mission statement. The preface to the 1866 *Book of Discipline* states:

> All their churches are required to be as free as the grace they preach. They believe that their mission is two-fold — to maintain the Bible standard of Christianity, and to preach the Gospel to the poor.

This two-fold mission has helped bring clarity to the mission where I currently serve. It has a vertical as well as a horizontal focus. The "Bible standard of Christianity" I take to be our historic doctrine of holiness of heart. We are to live and love like Jesus did. This is our vertical mission. To "preach the gospel to the poor" is our horizontal mission. It, too, is to live and love like Jesus.

In his presentation to the denominational Board of Administration a number of years ago, Dr. David McKenna connected this original mission to a vision for the future of Free Methodism. He proposed a new vertical-horizontal slogan for the 21$^{st}$ century — "a Passion for One and a Compassion for All."[1]

Our Lord's Great Commandment reflects the same dual thrust: "Love the Lord your God with all your heart, soul, mind, and strength." This is our vertical mission. The second is like it, "Love your neighbor as you love yourselves" — our horizontal mission. Vertical and horizontal, personal and social holiness, deep and wide — however we package it, it carries historical and biblical precedent. And, as I will try to prove, it remains as our most compelling witness to the world.

## The Pebble in Our Shoe

I am thankful for the leadership of our bishops these past

few years. I was on the Board of Administration when they composed the document, *Working Together in the 21st Century*.[2] They identified eight expected "outcomes" for our denominational mission along with ten statements that defined our community "culture." Without attempting to prioritize these outcomes and characteristics, I would still suggest two things about the two original "pillars" of our mission.

First, in the U.S. church, *these two pillars of our original mission — the doctrine of holiness and our special care for the poor — have become the most neglected of the eight outcomes*. What Albert Outler said about the United Methodist Church's neglect of holiness teaching could be said of us: "The keystone doctrine has become a pebble in her shoe." Likewise, the gospel to the poor has been relegated to a token seat at the table, overlooked among seemingly more pressing issues. We have a hand in charity work, but this is not what the founders had in mind when they spoke of preaching the Gospel to the poor.

Second, I would suggest that *it is precisely these two ideals that have the most potential of capturing the imagination of an unbelieving world*. The world is not impressed with our organizational image, our denominational heritage, our communication savvy, or even our cultural relevance. It is our life together in the radical way of Jesus that presents our most compelling witness.

## The First Pillar — Holiness

Over the course of my life, I have sat under various streams of holiness teaching. To be honest, I have often struggled to make sense of what I heard and witnessed. In a seminary class on the doctrine of entire sanctification, we memorized flow charts and lock-tight stages of faith. I remember the frustration I felt at the time, thinking: Could something so wondrous be so easily defined? Could something so dynamic be so easily "possessed"? I also wondered, how could something as life-giving as this so easily lend itself to dysfunctional religion?

More than twenty-five years later, I still have not found our classic and formulaic language to be very helpful. The gradual neglect of the doctrine across the church may indicate that there are others who have had the same difficulty. To their credit, our bishops have worked to bring the doctrine back into focus in the last few years. They might admit that the task is a challenging one. In exchange for an unsatisfying holiness, we seem to have inherited, over time, a confusing mix of traditions. In the past century, our loosely defined Wesleyan camp has adopted nuances of Western Calvinistic propositional evangelicalism ("Believe this and this and pray this prayer and you are saved"), popular market consumer religion, charismatic revivalism, ancient mysticism, fundamentalist legalism, passive universalism, and even modern pluralism. I wonder how many of our pastors, let alone our people, can discern the differences?

John Wesley described the work of salvation in comprehensive terms. He saw it as the "healing of the soul." The Hebrew vision was captured in the term, *shalom*. The Apostle Paul used the relational terms "reconciliation" and "adoption." Jesus simply called it *love* — "love God and love your neighbor as you love yourself." The metaphors he used were relational in every way — sheep to a shepherd, bride to a bridegroom, a child to a father.

### Beyond Abstinence, Status, and Separation

In the form it has been passed down, the doctrine of holiness can, I think, be summarized in three words: Abstinence, Status, and Separation. Let me explain what I mean and then suggest a dimension of holiness that goes beyond them.

1. *Beyond Abstinence.* Free Methodism still holds to a strong cultural value of abstinence. I would not argue against the importance of abstinence. Since our inception, we have stood against alcohol and drug use, all forms of gambling, sexual sin, and other abuses. Abstinence has served our community very well. It has provided the first line of protection for many. Some will remember that the issue of abstinence was what gave heat to the membership debate in the 1995 General Conference.

The problem with abstinence is not its value in setting behavioral boundaries for the community. The problem is its equation with the deeper work of holiness. Then holiness becomes defined by what it is *not* rather than what it so profoundly *is*. The holiness many of us inherited was defined by the cleansing of the heart from all that we are against!

Any recovered addict will tell you that abstinence is a vital component to recovery, but abstinence is not the ultimate goal. The opposite of addiction is not abstinence; it is something more. The goal of recovery is *community*. In fact, if we take the problem to its spiritual and psychological core, the opposite of sin and addiction and the goal of salvation is *intimacy* — reconciliation and intimacy with God and reconciliation and community with others. Hints of this are found in Genesis 2:25, the last word of pristine creation where the man and woman are fully known and yet completely safe: "The man and his wife were both naked, and they felt no shame." Or we hear Jesus' warning about demons who return to the house that is swept clean, but empty (Luke 11:24-27). We also find hints of such intimacy in Peter's word about love being sin's antidote: "Above all, love each other deeply, because love covers over a multitude of sins" (1 Peter 4:8).

2. *Beyond Status.* The holiness we inherited was described as an experience to be possessed, or a "state" to enter into. Others can unpack the finer points of the doctrine; I only suggest that this is where we find the breach in the doctrine where religious toxicity creeps in. The "state" to be achieved was too often understood to mean sinless perfection. Yet we have constantly backtracked on the words and the definitions. "Perfection" does not really mean "perfection." "Entire" is not entirely "entire." The "crisis experience" is both "instantaneous" and "gradual," and so forth. We are good at painting ourselves in and out of semantic corners.

The problem is, we simply cannot contain the dynamic of salvation in static terms. Jesus said, "Follow me." Jesus continues to be a moving target! If we take note of the relational metaphors of Jesus in defining salvation, and if we see *intimacy* as the antidote to sin, then we can see that holiness is relational as well.

In a relational context, new and helpful light is shed on the doctrine. A relationship cannot be defined as static, nor can it be arrived at "instantaneously." Wesleyan theologian Randy Maddox describes it more like a "dance" in which "God takes the first step but we must participate responsibly, lest the dance stumble or end."[3]

A few years ago I was teaching a class of ministerial students. One raised his hand to ask if I thought we would be "free" to sin once we were in heaven. It was a good question. I told him I could not presume to fully predict the nature of a mystery as great as heaven. According to my limited understanding of relationship, however, I can know that the goal of relationship is always love. What is more, the nature of love is always, by definition "free." Anything less than freedom is less than love.

So, after some thought, I said "Yes. I could be proven wrong, but it seems we will be free in heaven." The class went on to consider the possibility that we will likely be more free than we are now. It is sin that diminishes freedom, not holiness. It is to sin and the degenerate life that all static definitions belong. Holiness, however, is something else. It is freedom in the fullest sense. Freedom to do right, to love God — yes, that's easy enough.

I would also add, however, that holiness allows us the freedom to fail, freedom to more readily recognize sin in our hearts (How can you get better from something you're not allowed to have?), freedom to confess, freedom to make restitution, freedom to learn from our past rather than be incapacitated by guilt or locked in denial, freedom to try again, freedom to grow, freedom to "walk in the light as he is in the light," freedom to have "fellowship with each other," freedom from the nothingness of sin. John Wesley himself suggested, at least once, that growth in grace would continue throughout eternity.[4]

3. *Beyond "Separation."* I have been trying to find out whether there is any truth to an intriguing rumor that I heard about the small college/church community in which I currently live. Many decades ago, as it was told to me, the college

and church once marketed their utopia with the catch phrase, "Six Miles from the Nearest Sin"! No reliable source has verified the story, and the truth is probably not as interesting. Yet we would not find it difficult to believe that the sentiment, at least, was held by more than a few. For more than two-thirds of the past century, holiness was defined among Free Methodists primarily as "separation" from the world. Who can argue with that? After all, *separation* is the root meaning of the word.

A few years ago, I was browsing through the archived copies of the Young Peoples' Missionary Society (YPMS) newspaper in the Marston Memorial Historical Center. The cover story and picture in one issue featured a high school sophomore who refused to play the clarinet in her school band because they were to perform a Benny Goodman tune. I think the year was 1949. Her act of nonviolent resistance was celebrated as an exemplary witness for Christ. She was touted as a guardian of holiness among the up-and-coming generation. In 1949, there would have been little debate that this girl was the embodiment of the Free Methodist "Soul."

Just thirteen years later there was another group of believers gathered in the deep South, engaging in nonviolent resistance at the risk of their lives — not to protest a style of music, but to evoke the necessary "creative tension" to bring the cause of justice to the attention of an entire nation.

Which act of protest best captures the Free Methodist soul? Which cause would have most engaged the imagination of our founders?

The answer might be contained in this brief but most profound statement found in the preface to our *Book of Discipline*: "Free Methodists believe the best way to keep the world from invading the church is for the church to invade the world with redemptive purpose." If only we did.

*Abstinence, status*, and *separation*, left to themselves, have weighed down the message of holiness. Together they provide a gravitational pull away from healthy community and towards a privatized, isolationist religion. It is precisely at this point that the two pillars — holiness and a gospel for the poor — join together.

## The Second Pillar — Gospel for the Poor

Jim Wallis in his book *God's Politics: Why the Right Gets it Wrong and the Left Doesn't Get It*, offers a provocative review of the 2004 U.S. Presidential election. Both political parties went to their corners in the campaign year and raised the flag of moral values. The Republican platform focused on abortion and gay marriage as their "moral issues." The Democratic platform was less defined and lacked the rallying spiritual component so evident among the Republicans. They defined their moral cause in terms of championing the environment and issues of inclusion.

Neither ticket, however, provided any forceful challenge to the concept of pre-emptive war in Iraq. Neither provided any intelligible program to advocate for the poor. They perceived that these positions would not capture the interest of voters.[5]

Yet the cause of the poor is the predominant moral value in Scripture. And the loss of tens of thousands of lives to war in Iraq is a legitimate "life" issue, as Wallis notes. What is most troubling is that the Republican Party banked on having the conservative Christian majority in its corner. They guessed right. Moral and pro-life issues such as advocacy for the poor, caring for the environment, and challenging our nation's new policy towards war are not the main concerns of the conservative Christian majority in America. On the issues of abortion and the sanctity of marriage, we may be on task, but regarding the explicitly biblical issue of care for the poor, we have lost our soul.

In his ten-page "Letter from a Birmingham Jail," Martin Luther King Jr., responded to Birmingham clergy who made a public request to call off the civil rights marches in their town. He scribbled these prophetic words about the church in the margins of a newspaper —

> The contemporary church is often a weak, ineffectual voice with an uncertain sound. It is so often the arch supporter of the status quo. Far from being disturbed by the presence of the church, the power structure of the average community is consoled by the church's silent and often vocal sanction of things as they are.[6]

The second pillar of our early mission was to "preach the gospel to the poor." The founders would not have defined this as charity, but rather as inclusion and engagement on our part towards those whom society had left behind. The rental of pews, though now extinct in practice, still lives in principle.

In the 1800s, the rental of pews was an issue of access. The simple design of Free Methodist places of worship and the insistence of simple yet inspired worship without professional musicians were about accessibility to the poor. Early FM dress codes and the aversion to jewelry had little to do with the sin of adornment with bright colors (as was the case just forty years later). The point was to allow the poor to worship inconspicuously among us. Free Methodists were to serve, worship, and fellowship among the poor. The poor were not to receive alms as a sidelight to the church's mission; they were to receive preferential care and special sensitivity.[7] Accessibility and proximity to the poor clearly meant that Free Methodists were to abolish all separation and distinction within their congregations. It was not charity that they were to offer, but fellowship, advocacy, and justice.

It is one thing to be a Good Samaritan. It is another thing altogether to take in a beaten man to become your brother in Christ.

Most of our conversation about ministry to the poor today is confined to charity. This is the best we can do simply because we and our constituency, with our acquired social mobility, have effectively removed ourselves from the margins of society. Go to any metropolitan area and see churches tripping over each other to keep up with the green edges of suburban sprawl. Review the financial books of our churches and see the growing percentage of our resources given to staff and house our own ministries. Certainly a host of other dynamics lie behind the data, but we should ponder the dramatic increase in spending on staff and facilities among our U.S. churches over the last several years. Compare this trend with our relatively flat membership and convert growth, along with the minimal increase in our world missions giving (as illustrated in the chart at the end of this chapter).

What do these trends say about us? What does the increase in resources needed to staff and house our U.S. ministry reveal about our "soul"? Does it expose a materialism and consumerism among our people that is indistinct from the unbelieving population? Where is our "separation" from the values of the culture? Do these trends reflect the quality of our discipleship, of equipping our people astutely to challenge the predominant culture? Do our values and lifestyles stand in any way apart from the world? Have we lost our "soul"?

Robert Lewis, pastor of Fellowship Bible Church in Little Rock, Arkansas, has built a remarkable tradition of community service and redemptive influence as part of his church's small-group DNA. The church's philosophy of servant ministry is based on Matthew 5:16. It is a philosophy of engagement: "In the same way, let your light shine before others that they may see your good deeds and praise your Father in heaven."

In a culture that is increasingly cynical about the self-serving motives of the institutional church, Lewis' call for the Body of Christ to expend its energies and resources to selflessly and genuinely bless the surrounding community is a powerful witness.[8]

What the Fellowship Bible Church does goes far beyond the "Conspiracy of Kindness" model of the Cincinnati Vineyard Church. The latter can too easily be a cover for yet another form of marketing — a ploy that is not lost on critics of the church. Instead, "common cause" groups at Fellowship Bible Church are advocating for the poor, starting businesses, creating scholarships, providing housing, and mentoring young people.

Could this be the Free Methodist soul that we have lost? To love God in transparent humility, with all of our heart, soul, mind, and strength, and to love our neighbors *as much* as we love ourselves? Could we become a church that exists not to promote our own cause, ensure our own survival, or market our own distinctiveness? Can we instead become a church that exists solely to bless the world — to bring the preserving salt and light of the Gospel and the "shalom" of justice and peace wherever our people live, work, and play?

This is just my own take on the "Free Methodist soul." But could we gather Free Methodists from across the country, if not the whole world, around a some kind of consensus vision — a common "soul"? And if such a thing were possible, could we then submit ourselves to the radical transformation necessary to see such a "soul" take shape?

At least we have begun the conversation. The Spirit comes and goes as he pleases, but what pleases the Spirit is certainly much the same today as it was 150 years ago. Through the careful reading of the Scriptures, a thorough study of the lessons of history, and the astute analysis of our time, we may find the main path again.

May the Lord lead us together to a better vision than what any one of us could prescribe.

## Endnotes

[1] David L. McKenna, "Timely Heritage, Timeless Hope," address given to the Board of Administration, Indianapolis, October 28, 1997.

[2] *Working Together in the 21st Century*, pamphlet published by Free Methodist Communications, 2002.

[3] Randy Maddox, *Responsible Grace* (Kingswood, 1994), 151–152. Maddox suggests that such a "dance" conveys a process that takes place over time. Wesley embraced an Eastern Christian as well as a Western view of salvation. The Eastern view sees salvation as a therapeutic transformation. Western understandings of salvation focused more on a legal act of pardon, a momentary transaction. In his later years, Wesley avoided the term "conversion." In his opinion, "God's typical manner of working in all areas of providence and grace was gradual" (Maddox, 152). The issue of instantaneous sanctification versus gradual process has been debated for generations. The point here is, when seen in its proper relational context (as opposed to a "static" one) the dynamics of salvation become quite clear.

[4] See Maddox, *Responsible Grace*, 152; John Wesley, "Father Thoughts Upon Christian Perfection," Q. 29, *The Works of John Wesley* (Jackson), 11:426.

[5] Jim Wallis, *God's Politics* (Harper, 2005). In 2004, Republicans as well as Democrats voted overwhelmingly according to "moral

issues." Same-sex marriage and abortion were the predominant "moral issues" of the conservative vote. In a number of key states, a same-sex constitutional amendment was placed on the ballot — a strategic device that greatly aided Republican turnout. A week after the election, however, a poll conducted by Zogby International found that when "a broader and more specific list of moral issues was presented, the results were quite different. When asked 'Which moral issue most influenced your vote?' 42 percent chose the war in Iraq while 13 percent said abortion, and 9 percent said same-sex marriage. When asked to choose the most urgent moral problem in American culture, 33 percent selected greed and materialism; 31 percent, poverty and economic justice; 16 percent abortion; and 12 percent, same-sex marriage. The 'greatest threat to marriage' was identified as infidelity by 31 percent, rising financial burdens by 25 percent, and same-sex marriage by 22 percent." Wallis, xvii.

[6] Martin Luther King Jr., "Letter from a Birmingham Jail," April 16, 1963 (From www.historicaltextarchive.com, 2003).

[7] B.T. Roberts, "Free Churches," *The Earnest Christian* 1:1 (January 1860), 6-10.

[8] Robert Lewis, *The Church of Irresistible Influence* (Zondervan, 2001), 63-64.

## Selected Statistical Profile of Free Methodism, 2000-2002
Free Methodist *Yearbook* (U.S. conferences only)

|  | 2000 | 2001 | 2002 |
|---|---|---|---|
| Membership* | 72,425 | 71,308 | 71,225 |
| Attendance | 90,303 | 91,376 | 94,053 |
| Cost of church staffing: | | | |
| Senior Pastor | $15,517,541 | $15,642,404 | $16,096,123 |
| Pastoral Housing | 6,710,039 | 6,963,714 | 7,469,294 |
| Pastoral Benefits | 6,491,554 | 6,709,625 | 6,972,061 |
| Other Appt. Staff | 4,323,356 | 4,778,250 | 4,984,941 |
| Staff Housing | 2,024,655 | 2,317,167 | 2,693,841 |
| Staff Benefits | 1,616,248 | 1,877,204 | 2,140,720 |
| Capital Improvement | 15,576,060 | 21,640,926 | 29,049,741 |
| **Total Expenditure** | **$52,259,453** | **$59,929,290** | **$69,406,721** |
| World Missions** | $3,128,499 | 3,314,793 | 3,369,943 |

Note: The 2003 and 2004 yearbooks revised the categories of their data. The trend from 2000 to 2002, however, shows a 33 percent increase in spending on staff and capital improvements across the U.S. church. In the same time period, UMC giving increased 7.7 percent while total membership in the U.S. decreased by 1.7 percent.

*Membership includes all adult (except for ordained ministers), preparatory, junior, and ministerial membership.

**World Missions UMC only. Does not include non-UMC or non-FM missions giving.

## CHAPTER 5
# *Learning from Brazilian Free Methodism*

José Ildo Mello Swartele de Mello
Bishop, Free Methodist Church of Brazil
São Paulo, Brazil

The church needs a genuine revival to faithfully fulfill its call to be the salt and light of this world.

Jesus said in Matthew 13:31-32:

*The kingdom of heaven is like a mustard seed, which a man took and planted in his field. Though it is the smallest of all seeds, yet when it grows, it is the largest of garden plants and becomes a tree, so that the birds come and perch in its branches.*

A few years ago a pastor of another denomination was invited to preach in a special meeting about the mission of our FM Brazilian Conference. Knowing that our motto for that year was "Prayer and Action for a Better World," he began by saying: "Prayer and action, yes; but a better world, no!" We don't have to nourish hope about this condemned world before Jesus' second coming, he said. For him, the mission of the church was like Noah's ark. It is confined to preaching the gospel to save souls.

That kind of theology makes preachers merely ominous foreboders of the end. The thinking is: The worse it gets, the better it is, because that means that Jesus is coming. From this point of view, the kingdom of God is solely future. It begins in a radical and abrupt way with Jesus' second coming. Accommodation and escapism are the unavoidable consequences.

So what *is* the kingdom of God? Let's examine the way Jesus and the Apostles understood God's kingdom.

### The Reality of God's Reign

Jesus often taught that the manifestation and establishment of God's kingdom is a slow, gradual process with a small and modest beginning. God's kingdom is not like an abrupt volcanic eruption; its like to a mustard seed in its gradual process of growing. The beginning is small, small as a little group of disciples, as in Jesus' day!

We must not despise the power of such small mustard seeds! Like a tiny seed, the kingdom of God is destined to grow and spread influence as salt of the earth and light of the world. As Christians, our presence here is to promote light, hope, justice, and life as agents of God's reign. "Let your light shine before others, that they may see your good deeds and glorify your Father in heaven" (Mt. 5:16), Jesus taught.

The kingdom of God has already been initiated in this world. Jesus said, "If it is by the Spirit of God that I drive out demons, then the kingdom of God is come upon you" (Mt. 12:28). As Christians, we understand that Jesus was in fact casting out devils by the Spirit of God — which, Jesus says, is a sign that the kingdom of God is come to us.

Note that Jesus speaks here of the kingdom of God in terms of *this present age*, here and now! In verse 29, Jesus continues this point by asking a question: "How can anyone enter a strong man's house and carry off his possessions without first tying up the strong man? Then his house can be plundered." Perhaps Jesus' statement here casts light on the controversial text in Revelation 20 that speaks about the binding and imprisonment of Satan. In this connection, note also what Paul says about Jesus' victory in Ephesians 1:20–23 and 2:6. God

> raised Christ from the dead and seated him at his right hand in the heavenly realms, far above all rule and authority, power and dominion, and every name that can be invoked, not only in the present age but also in the one to come. And God placed all things under his feet and appointed him to be head over everything for the church, which is his body, the fullness of him who fills everything in every way.
>
> ... And God raised us up with Christ and seated us with him in the heavenly realms in Christ Jesus.

We see in Matthew 12:28–29 that Jesus was casting out devils. He was spoiling the goods of the strong man's house — which Jesus could do because he first took care to bind the strong man. This pictures the truth that the kingdom of God is come to this world. Being tied or bound doesn't mean that Satan ceases to exercise power and influence, but it does means he was fatally wounded by the birth, life, death and resurrection of the legitimate King of this world — the Lord Jesus, who came to this world to destroy the works of the devil (1 John 3:8).

The Second World War gives us a good illustration. There was a difference between the final battle and the decisive battle. The famous D-Day invasion was the decisive battle. After that day, although the enemy continued fighting, he was fatally wounded. Military experts knew there was no hope for him.

Since Jesus came, Satan is bound in the sense that he no longer has the power and freedom to block the progress of the church's mission. Jesus said, "On this rock I will build my church, and the gates of death will not overcome it" (Mt. 16:18). Satan continues opposing God's kingdom, but his power is now restricted to the point that the "gates of death" or hell cannot stop the mission of the church.

Jesus said the gospel of the kingdom would be preached in the whole world as a testimony to all nations before the end comes (Mt. 24:14). This means the church will succeed in the great mission Jesus has given it. Similarly, we see in Luke 10:18-19 that Jesus' disciples were glad they were able to cast out demons as Jesus had done. Jesus said, "I saw Satan fall like lightning from heaven. I have given you authority to trample on snakes and scorpions and to overcome all the power of the enemy; nothing will harm you."

The Apostles recognized the triumph of Christ on the cross. Paul wrote that Jesus "having disarmed the powers and authorities ... made a public spectacle of them, triumphing over them by the cross" (Col. 2:15). And the final battle awaits the return Jesus Christ when death, the last enemy, will fully be put under the feet of the Lord. Until then we have to fight the good fight (2 Tim. 4:7). Paul's declaration in 1 Corinthians 15:25-26 that Jesus "must reign until he has put all his enemies under his feet" can be understood only in terms of the present age, before Jesus' triumphant return, because only then will death, "the last enemy," be destroyed. Jesus' second coming marks the end and not the beginning of this period of God's reign in this world.

Paul says in Colossians 1:13 that God "has rescued us from the dominion of darkness and brought us into the kingdom of the Son he loves." We must not forget that the earliest and most basic declaration of Christian faith is "Jesus is Lord." This has many implications, including social and political ones. Many Christians died because of this "simple" confession. It means much more than saying that Jesus is the Lord of my life — it means that he is the Lord of the whole world. That's why he is called the King of kings!

What do we think when we pray what Jesus taught us, "your kingdom come, your will be done on earth as it is in heaven"? Did Jesus mean the here and now in this age, or only the future after his return? Doesn't Jesus teach us that, instead of being anxious about material things, we must seek *now* his kingdom and its righteousness and justice (Mt. 6:33)? What must a Christian do with the hunger and thirst for righteousness that must characterize a child of God (Mt. 5:6)?

## Present Hope for God's Kingdom

John Wesley was optimistic about the sufficiency of the power of the grace of Jesus not only to forgive our sins but also to purify us from all unrighteousness and transform us into new creatures who are able to be imitators of God as dearly loved children. And Wesley didn't stop there. He also believed in the power of this grace to transform the whole world. Wesley reportedly once said: "Give me a hundred men who love nothing but God and hate nothing but sin, and I will shake the whole world for Christ. It doesn't matter if they are clerics or lay, men like that will beat the kingdom of Satan and will build the kingdom of God on earth."

John Wesley "saw God's grace so fully abounding that one could not set limits on what God's Spirit might accomplish through the church in the present order," notes Howard

Snyder in *The Radical Wesley*. But "this emphasis had to be combined with the warning of judgment and eternal punishment. Biblical realism required holding together eschatological hope and dread" (*The Radical Wesley*, 146, 85).

Jesus continues his teaching about the nature of his kingdom in this age, saying that the kingdom of God grows as good seed, but the enemy plants weeds. A conflict exists between the forces of the enemy and those of God. The enemy is trying to obstruct the expansion of God's kingdom purposes. This war will continue until the last battle, when the last enemy will be put under Jesus' feet.

John Wesley didn't ignore the prophecies that speak about the great distress, the apostasy of many Christians and the increase of wickedness at the end of the time. But he saw these prophecies combined in the same context where Jesus also says that the church will succeed in accomplishing its mission, for "this gospel of the kingdom will be preached in the whole world as a testimony to all nations, and then the end will come" (Mt. 24:14). But Wesley's realism did not lessen his motivation nor the optimism that moved him to action. He never lost his idealism, which was based on his confidence in the power of God for personal and social sanctification and transformation. His eschatology (view of last things) did not permit him to merely rest in a position of contemplation. "Why do you stand here looking into the sky?" the angels asked Jesus' disciples in Acts 1:10.

Wesley's eschatology did not focus on speculation. The purpose of biblical teachings on the last days is not to satisfy our curiosity. So Wesley did not just look forward to the final day of the Lord; he also worked very hard to speed the coming of Jesus, as Peter exhorted us to do (2 Peter 3:12). Wesley knew that Jesus' second coming was tied to the fulfillment of the church's mission. "The Lord is not slow in keeping his promise, as some understand slowness. Instead he is patient with you, not wanting anyone

> John Wesley's biblical realism did not lessen his optimism about God's grace in the present world.

to perish, but everyone to come to repentance" (2 Peter 3:9).

Wesley understood that the New Testament combines the evangelistic and the prophetic dimensions of the gospel in the same package. No split between personal salvation and social engagement. Wesley believed with Paul that the faith which saves is the faith that expresses itself through love (Gal. 5:6).

So we today are sent in mission to this world just as the Father sent Jesus (John 20:21). We recall again 1 John 3:8, "The reason the Son of God appeared was to destroy the devil's work." We remember "how God anointed Jesus of Nazareth with the Holy Spirit and power, and how he went around doing good and healing all who were under the power of the devil, because God was with him" (Acts 10:38). Jesus was concerned not only about the human soul; he showed concern for the whole person and the whole of life. His ministry of compassion was not merely bait for fishing souls. Some people who were healed by Jesus ended up not following him. Some didn't even return to say thank you. We see from Jesus' example that the ministry of compassion has value in and of itself. It belongs to the essential nature of the God's kingdom, which is love! Jesus cannot deny himself. What about us?

Wesley was a man of conviction. For him, theology and practice really were one! David McKenna writes in his book *What a Time to be Wesleyan*, "As a logical consequence of the Arminian doctrine of unlimited atonement, Wesley preached the natural rights of all [people] for social as well as spiritual freedom" (p. 99). Wesley dared to believe that the world could be improved by the grace of God. Imagine what it was like to be living in the time of Wesley and to decide to work to change such a deep social evil as slavery. Utopia?! The last letter John Wesley wrote was to William Wilberforce, a young Member of Parliament. Expressing his opposition to slavery and the slave trade, Wesley encouraged Wilberforce to take action for change. Parliament finally outlawed England's participation in the slave trade years after Wesley's death.

The status quo does not have the last word. There is hope! Who knows what could have happened if the Methodist church had not declined spiritually in the decades following Wesley's death? Perhaps Karl Marx would not have said "Religion is the opiate of the people." Perhaps Marx wouldn't have been prompted by his social context to write his thesis. Who can say how many wars, how much racism and how many social injustices could have been avoided if the church had always been faithful to the call of the Gospel!

For example, how powerful could our testimony have been to a fragmented world about the love, peace and unity we can experience in Christ if the church had not succumbed to the status quo, adopting a philosophy of church growth based in homogeneity — a principle so prevalent in our segregated culture? It doesn't matter that this principle works. Of course it works, because it makes it easy for people who don't want to cross social and ethnic barriers.

Such pragmatism doesn't break with the evil structures that divide people into social classes and ethnic groups. How can a segregated church say to a segregated and divided world that the final purpose of God is the unity of all things in Christ? It will be possible only if we can say with Paul: "Here [in the church] there is no Greek or Jew, circumcised or uncircumcised, barbarian, Scythian, slave or free, but Christ is all, and is in all" (Col. 3:11)! Could the ignominious apartheid in South Africa been have avoided? What about the racism in other "evangelical" countries? Unfortunately the great revival that happened in Rwanda and Burundi did not reach the necessary depth to destroy the barriers and the dividing wall of hostility that exists between Hutus and Tutsis, which could have prevented that tremendous genocide.

> How can a segregated church say to a segregated and divided world that the final purpose of God is the unity of all things in Christ?

Another implication of this criticism of the "principle" of homogeneity — less critical, but still important — concerns music in the church. Many people have abandoned churches that will not accept even a combination of traditional and contemporary musical styles. These people show their intolerance. They sanctify what is secondary to the detriment of what is primary: the holiness of our unity in Christ. Some people reveal an extreme zeal for particular music styles, a zeal that should be given instead to love. The New Testament says almost nothing about musical styles, but speaks a lot about the unity of the body of Christ and the love that must drive our relationships. "Love is patient, love is kind. It does not envy, ... is not self-seeking, ... it always perseveres" (1 Cor. 13:4-7). To promote the unity of the church, shouldn't "we who are strong ... bear the failings of the weak and not [seek] to please ourselves" (Rom. 15:1)? Paul reminds us of the necessity of "bearing with one another in love" (Eph. 4:2).

Dividing a congregation into two groups is not the way to solve the conflict. This just bears witness that that which divides us is stronger than the love that should join us.

Another basic consideration is our mission to reach the lost. The church doesn't live for itself. In thinking about church worship services and meetings, we must consider the opinion of unbelievers, as Paul teaches (1 Cor. 14:23). In such secondary matters, we must be ready to give up our own preferences in order to see people saved. Because "one soul is worth more than the whole world," John and Charles Wesley sacrificed personal preferences and esthetic tastes in order to reach the lost. The principle here is *kenosis*: the self-emptying (Phil. 2:7) of one's own cultural tastes. Charles Wesley was a cultured poet and a musician with refined taste, but he chose to write hymns as simple and common as those sung in the English taverns. And John Wesley, after thirty-three years of preaching in the open air, confessed it was still a cross for him.

What sacrifices are we making in the name of love and to promote the unity and the mission of the church?

John Wesley also fought for fair prices and wages, a safe work environment, and prison reform. He opposed unjust wars, the production and consumption of alcohol, and child labor. All this for the sake of mission.

We live in a world of materialism. Satan is the lord of materialism. Paul said "the love of money is a root of all kinds of evil" (1 Tim. 6:10). We are constantly bombarded by the media that wants us to conform to a way of life where people work to earn, earn to buy, and buy to prove their value. Concerns about social status, worry about consuming and possessing, about insurance and the future — all these have deeply undermined a profound commitment to God's will.

The Bible says, "Do not love the world" (1 John 2:15) — that is, the world system and its values. "Do not conform to the pattern of this world, but be transformed by the renewing of your mind. Then you will be able to test and approve what God's will is — his good, pleasing and perfect will" (Rom. 12:2). "Do not store up for yourselves treasures on earth. ... No one can serve two masters" (Mt. 6:19, 24). Believers react against the threat of Communism but then end up surrendering to capitalism, failing to perceive the evil of seeking self-gratification in the pleasures of this world, the never-ending drive for consumption, materialism and individualism. Prosperity theology is just an extreme manifestation of the greater problem of a lack of vision for the kingdom of God among evangelicals. It seems we have lost the pilgrim mentality.

The book *Money, Possessions and Eternity* by Randy Alcorn shows what the Bible teaches on this subject. The ultimate answer to the problem is a genuine revival that fills our hearts with love and moves us to simpler living so we can give more and more to the poor and to the church — a revival that moves us to seek first God's kingdom and righteousness. As a small seed, this revival can start with one person or with a small group of believers who are ready to obey all the commandments of the Lord.

## Grace-filled Living

For John Wesley, giving grace was the final evidence of the Spirit-filled life. Grace freely received must be grace freely given. If not, it risks being canceled by the King (Mt. 18:25-34). David McKenna in his wonderful book *What a Time to Be a Wesleyan!* says, "Against the great social corruption of England, Wesley lived out the fruit of the Spirit. Although he became one of the richest men in England, he lived annually on 28 pounds until his death, giving away the rest to the poor" (p. 41).

How can believers be united in mission if some of them live in an ostentatious way? Rampant poverty in the world puts a question mark on the lifestyles of many Christians. What must we do? We must follow the example of Jesus, the apostles, Wesley, and Francis Asbury, among others. Simple living and the practice of charity in the gracious spirit of Christ is what impacts the world. Note that the sign of the salvation of Zacchaeus was that he spontaneously decided to share his money. In contrast, the ambition for money was the sign of condemnation to the rich young man. The most powerful sign of Pentecost was that the multitude of disciples showed love and care toward each other. These first disciples "had everything in common. They sold property and possessions to give to anyone who had need" (Acts 2:44-45).

Is the gospel good news for the poor only in terms of the promise of eternity in heaven? Weren't the poor of the early church experiencing the firstfruits of the justice of the kingdom? Remember that in the Old Testament the Jubilee year was good news to the poor. But only Jesus at Pentecost was able to accomplish the year of Jubilee. Pentecost was a type of agrarian reformation, a communism promoted not by power, but by the Spirit of Jesus.

"But this is impossible nowadays," someone will argue. Jesus would answer: "With human beings this is impossible, but not with God; all things are possible with God" (Mark 10:27).

So truly we need a revival! Revival is the discovery of original values and principles. We must look back to see if there are key values we have forgotten.

Small groups can be one way of building revival fires. Small groups can help develop sanctified Christian character and other values of the kingdom of God. Holy living must be nurtured in the community of the converted that desires to walk as Jesus did. Men and women are social beings. One influences the other, mainly by example. If we want to change individuals and society, we must develop small groups that can taste the goodness of the Word of God and the power of the coming age.

Methodism lost this vision that was so vital for Wesley. We in the Wesleyan tradition have neglected our precious legacy. Today, to our shame, other Christian churches are rediscovering the importance of small groups. Vital groups help us remember that *the kingdom of heaven is like to a grain of mustard seed*! The power of the progress and impact of these micro-contexts is impressive. This is the strategy of the kingdom!

A revival produces growth. In America, the informality and dynamism of the Wesleyan movement caused the new Methodist church to grow from 15,000 members in 1780 to 1,360,000 members by 1850. The Methodist Episcopal Church became by far the largest denomination on American soil, followed by the Baptists with 800,000, the Presbyterians with 460,000 and the Episcopalians with 200,000.

We need to return to our roots. We need a Wesleyan-style revival; to experience what they experienced and to produce similar fruit. Revivals today are not what they used to be. Revivals became evangelistic campaigns or services charged with emotion, often with the stamp of self-centeredness and individualism on them. Such campaigns and services often are concerned with the transcendent exclusively. They are strong on promotion, pressure, and emotion, but weak on biblical content and lacking in prophetic depth. Such "revivals" hide the price of discipleship in the attempt to please the customer. They are unable to guide people into denying self in order to place themselves entirely under the lordship of Jesus Christ.

In much popular evangelism, the decision to "accept Christ" is simply the means by which people achieve the "good life" without paying any price. The cross loses its shame — it points to the sacrifice that Jesus Christ made for us, but is not a call to discipleship. It is the cross of Christ exclusively, not of the disciple, not of cross-bearing discipleship. The God of this Christianity is the God of "cheap grace," the God who always gives, never demanding anything; the God made for the person who lives by the rule of the least resistance.

## The Revival We Need

The manipulation of the gospel for personal success will

always lead to slavery to the world and its powers. We need a revival like the early Wesleyan movement, a revival that moves us to holistic mission, driving us to live and preach all that Jesus taught. A revival that keeps us from worrying only about the salvation of the soul while ignoring the physical needs. We need a revival that not only promotes reconciliation with God but also reconciliation among people. A revival that promotes deep repentance — not psychological and emotional relief of a guilty conscience, but the acceptance of the cross as a death to this world with the purpose of living for God. If Jesus is Lord, then persons must be confronted with his authority over the totality of life.

> If Jesus is Lord, then people must be confronted with his authority over all of life.

God is doing great things among us in Brazil. But when I think about what God did in the times of Wesley, Asbury and B.T. Roberts, I am overcome by a sense of failure or insufficiency. But I still have a dream! Because we have this tremendous legacy, I dare to dream of taking part in a great revival, the greatest in all the history of the church — a revival that impacts this world with the power of the holy gospel of Jesus!

John Wesley is gone. How good it would be if he were here to help us. Could we make a Wesley clone? No, not a good idea — not just because of the ethical implications of cloning, but because the secret of Wesley's life was not primarily in his genes or academic formation. We need to remember that Wesley failed in his first mission to America. The secret of his fruitful ministry was the spiritual experience that changed his life and the world around him.

The God who moved remarkably in former days is still on his throne. "Lord, I have heard of your fame; I stand in awe of your deeds. Lord, Renew them in our day, in our time make them known; in wrath remember mercy" (Hab. 3:2).

O Lord, revive your work in our day! "Do it again, Lord!"

## CHAPTER 6
# Free Methodist Mission: Justice — "To Break Every Yoke"

John Hay Jr.
Pastor, West Morris Street Free Methodist Church
Indianapolis, Indiana

"He has told you, O man, what is good; and what does the LORD require of you but to do justice, to love kindness, and to walk humbly with your God" (Micah 6:8, *NASB*)?

"Every church seeking justice and showing mercy to the poor and disenfranchised" ("Profile of a Healthy Church," Free Methodist Mission Statement, 2003).

As a local pastor and participant in Wesleyan/holiness movement ecclesiology today, this is my question: *What place ought "doing justice" to have in the common ministry life of a Free Methodist believer, pastor, and congregation?*

I explore this question here and live it in my life as a pastor. It should not be quickly or easily answered, for the conclusion determines whether or not "doing justice" will have a greater or lesser place in preaching, planning, resource allocation, servant leadership, community engagement, and volunteer investment and deployment in a local setting.

What place *should* "doing justice" have in the common ministry life of a Free Methodist believer, pastor, and congregation? However difficult the question, *it should be answered* — with conviction and subsequent action. If it is determined that "doing justice" should have only a secondary place, then let us get on with what it is felt that this branch of the body of Christ is supposed to be doing and developing at local levels, and let us fan the flame of "doing justice" that we feel is more appropriately located outside the parish setting. If it is determined, however, that justice should have a more central place in the life of believers, pastors, and local congregations, then the urgency of pressing biblical justice issues in contemporary American society and on the global stage compels us to engage unhesitatingly, wholeheartedly, and unflinchingly.

Our 147-year history of published books, periodicals, articles, conference minutes and an ever-evolving *Book of Discipline* make it clear that "doing justice" has robust meaning among Free Methodists. This was particularly so in the years before the onset of the Fundamentalist-Modernist controversy. The abolition of slavery and open access to (if not outright preference for) the poor are two justice issues that were part and parcel of the formation of the Free Methodist Church in 1860. Early Free Methodists advocated intensively and insistently for the freedom of all human beings and free access for the poor at every level of the church. (See chapter 2, above.)

A continuing thread of emphasis on justice characterized in official Free Methodist documents and periodicals up to the present. Granted, this thread has been sometimes Spartan. For instance, new Free Methodists being oriented to membership with the 1978 book *Belonging!* would have had little inkling that doing justice was a part of the denomination's history or current interest. But any pastor reading the 1998 edition of the *Pastor's Handbook* would be moved by the passion for justice expressed in a twelve-point statement co-authored by Bishop Gerald Bates and Howard Olver titled "A Social Urban and Ethnic Agenda for the Free Methodist Church in the Nineties." More recently, the 2003 denomination-wide mission statement includes in the local profile of a healthy congregation: "Every church seeking justice and showing mercy to the poor and disenfranchised."

Without question, the history and challenge of "doing justice" is well-embedded in our denominational DNA. The precedents and practices are ample. The more pressing question, to me, is this: What range should "doing justice" have in the life of a believer, a pastor, and a local congregation today? And in what forms?

My inclination is to assert that doing justice should have a more central place in my life as a believer, my leadership as a pastor, and our common life as a Free Methodist congregation than it does. Explicit acts of doing justice are more exceptional than common. Justice-doing is set apart from the spiritual disciplines and service priorities of most Wesleyan/holiness believers, pastors, and congregations. This heightens the urgency and complexity of the question.

Could it be that we know justice is *not* being done and we know that it *should* be done, but we don't believe it is the role of the individual believer, local pastor, or local community of faith to be concerned with justice as a matter of principle or priority? Perhaps we believe justice *should* be done, but that church growth, evangelism, conversion, discipleship, and membership development are more important. Will we then "do justice" after we get these other ministry priorities well underway? Will we get around to it? Do we feel that adequate justice is being done through these other priorities?

Or do we leave justice to specialized ministries within our congregations, to organizations represented in the Association of Human Service Ministries (AHSM) of the Free Methodist Church, to parachurch organizations, to political influence groups supposedly acting in the best interests of Christianity, or to secular justice advocacy groups? In other words, do we believe that "doing justice" is a specialized ministry and not a central imperative for local believers, pastors, and congregations?

Or do we follow what seems to have become the dominant practice of most Wesleyan/holiness believers, pastors, and congregations (following the lead of many contemporary evangelical churches): Revert to letting acts of charity, compassion, mercy, and philanthropy supplant or substitute for the biblical mandate to do justice? If it is appropriate to "show mercy" in parish ministry, why is it not equally appropriate to do justice in this setting? Are we satisfied to provide local, national, and international relief for the oppressed and support philanthropic care for those who are repeatedly wounded by society's injustices? Or shall we really engage the imperative of Isaiah 58: "loose the chains of injustice and untie the cords of the yoke," "set the oppressed free and break every yoke," "do away with the yoke of oppression," "spend [ourselves] on behalf of the hungry and satisfy the needs of the oppressed"?

I have found Harvie Conn's definition of evangelism most helpful as I reflect on ministry as a Wesleyan/holiness pastor in an urban setting. Echoing New Testament teachings, Conn says emphatically: "Evangelism is preaching grace and doing justice." This combination, which Conn likens to two oars necessary to row a boat upstream, is reflected in Wesley's Methodists and in early Free Methodism.

> Old Testament Hebrew understandings of justice are more about relationships among people than about legal questions.

If we can clarify what "doing justice" means, maybe we can better assess its historic place in Free Methodism and in local Free Methodist ministry today. Here are some biblical and theological underpinnings that help me focus the terms and question.

**Biblical Foundations for Doing Justice**

Isaiah 58 goes a long way to contextually define "doing justice." Here, as in most other Old Testament references, justice is about fairness for the oppressed, right relationships in the marketplace, remuneration for inequitable treatment, and opportunity to stand on common ground.

While the later Greek terms for justice are more legally defined, these earlier Hebrew understandings of justice are more about relationships between people. I am convinced that one challenge in "doing justice" today is the overwhelmingly Greco-Roman interpretations of justice that dominate the Western worldview. But the words and imagery in Isaiah 58 are not legal or punitive. These images are unmistakable: slaves' chains are to be loosed and slaves emancipated; people treated like oxen under a tightly-tied yoke are to be released and every instrument of control, manipulation, and abuse broken.

Message: *"do away with the yoke of oppression."* Application: slavery, human trafficking, permanent economic subjection, and advantage-taking of laborers is unjust and must cease. Isaiah's concern is that the people of God, if they are to be a people who reflect who God is and if they are to be *blessed* by God, will do business in radical distinction from what other people try to get by with.

Isaiah 58 also helps us distinguish *justice* from *mercy*. Verse 6 calls for actions that permanently change social norms and reform economic practices. Verse 7 however calls more for mercy and hospitality: "share your food with the hungry," "provide the poor wanderer with shelter," and clothe the naked. *Acts of mercy* are needed to relieve immediate crises and human indignities. *Acts of justice* are needed to prevent or rectify the crises and indignities that are repeatedly visited upon vulnerable individuals and groups.

Mercy and hospitality bring us into a relieving relationship with neighbors in distress, while seeking justice brings us into solidarity with oppressed neighbors and into a transformation of policies, practices, and structures that once directly harmed them and simultaneously forfeited the spiritual integrity of people called to reflect God's character.

Many Christians seem to lump justice and mercy together and separate both from the message of salvation and the call to kingdom living. Isaiah 58 is one of several Old and New Testament passages that will neither allow us to merge justice and mercy nor disconnect justice and mercy from salvation and faithfulness as a covenant people. Faith in God is connected to faithfulness to neighbors in our daily personal and marketplace practices. Personal salvation is linked to corporate, community, and international policies, with the bottom-line question being: "what does it do to the poor?"

The Bible's collective witness to doing justice was certainly on the minds and hearts, and seen in the actions, of our theological and denominational forebears. Biblical references to justice were not something for academic debate and genteel discussion and then left for optional or occasional action. When read with an immediate awareness of the poor, oppressed, distressed, de-

> In the Bible, personal salvation is linked to corporate, community, and international policies — and how they affect the poor.

nied, marginalized, and disregarded, the Bible's many passages calling for justice in response to the poor, laborers, aliens, slaves, women, and prisoners became a prophetic testimony against the dominant culture and careless practices of the church. The biblical call to do justice was read, proclaimed, and applied with a literalness and urgency that animated the Wesleys and, later, the Robertses and others. In the face of glaring injustices, early Methodist and Free Methodist leaders saw God's Word being just as scandalized as were the poor. To ignore issues of social justice where they were clearly declared and previously judged in the Word of God was a form of rebellion against God.

**Theological Underpinnings for Doing Justice**

Some historians have argued that our Wesleyan/holiness forebears should be seen less as accomplished theologians and more as motivated ethical activists. While some theologians laud the theological brilliance of Wesley and the 19th-century holiness proclaimers, Donald Dayton (in "The Holiness Churches: A Significant Ethical Tradition") and Timothy Smith (in *Revivalism and Social Reform*) shine revealing light on the social and ethical impacts of these movements. As Wesleyans connected basically sound theology with pressing issues of social justice, new patterns of spiritual formation were developed and social renewal resulted.

One of my mentors, the Nazarene theologian Wesley D. Tracy, taught me that the initial formation and application of core holiness theology must be understood within the context of social injustice that existed in England in the mid-18th century. Imagine the impact that the Arminian teaching that *all may be saved* had on people in the slums and mining communities — people who had received the message from the dominant church that they were (as evidenced by their self-destructive behavior) predestined to hell. Imagine the impact John Wesley's preaching on *assurance* had on people made to fear daily for their very lives and livelihoods. Imagine the effect that the focus on *adoption* had on those whose social standing was nonexistent. Imagine the power of an ecclesiology that actualized the *priesthood of all believers*, regardless of formal training or official credentialing.

First among teachings that fed the "habits of the heart" of the early Methodists was the doctrine of Christian perfection. Imagine the hope for England's poor that was conveyed in Wesley's teaching that God's grace is sufficient to empower a person to live the fullness and integrity of life that God intends. That God is able to impart sin-defeating, heart-changing love; to lead one by the Holy Spirit in a life-long relationship of being transformed into the likeness of Jesus. This was Good News indeed. And when the possibility of being *personally* whole is raised and realized, then the possibility of a community or society being *corporately* whole — just, fair, equitable, what it is intended to be — is also raised. If it is possible at a personal level to love God completely and one's neighbor as oneself, this raises the possibility of glorifying God and loving neighbors together in a community and systems in which justice, mercy, and truth prevail over injustice, insensitivity, and corruption born of deception, relativism, cynicism and raw self-interest. Such is the optimism borne of grace.

Imagine the combination of these teachings woven together into the fabric of the early Methodist societies as living communities in witness to a world rife with sanctioned injustice and routine social oppression. Theologically speaking, injustice may well be the very irritant around which the pearl of holiness theology is formed. Given this formation, it would seem that through attempting to embody and bring about justice today the holiness churches may most brightly shine.

> **Theologically speaking, injustice may well be the very irritant around which the pearl of holiness theology is formed.**

It was no accident that the Wesleys and the early Methodists saw so many people personally transformed and affected significant social reform within a generation. Reforms in England at the time are striking. Under the slogan "join hands with God to help a poor man live," Wesley and his spiritual descendants pushed through such laws as the Factory Acts,

Miners Acts, and the Child Labor Laws. Methodists led in labor organizing. The Methodist emphases on education and economic opportunity were socially developmental: literacy, health education, family counsel, financial guidance, revolving loan funds, and small business incubators, along with an insistence on temperance, chastity, and personal integrity. In light of this, we begin to understand the larger cultural implications of what Wesley meant when he said "there is no holiness but social holiness."

### Free Methodist Expressions of Justice

Likewise, a century later in America, it was no stretch of biblical or theological application for B.T. Roberts and the Free Methodists to directly address human slavery and poverty. These injustices and others — denial of the rights of women, the plight of farmers, and unjust economic policies of the state — were not beyond the scope of core Christian experience, the church's concerns and the activities of its leaders. In *Populist Saints,* Howard Snyder demonstrates how clearly Roberts grasped the connection between heart holiness and social justice. He reflected it in the mainstream of his writing, speaking and organizing.

Like other holiness groups, Free Methodists rallied around the often quoted statement of Phoebe Palmer: "Pentecost laid the axe at the root of social injustice." Dayton points out that holiness group involvements with the oppressed were "much more than just 'relief' efforts." Their contact with the poor led them "toward new social and political positions that favored the oppressed. Some," Dayton notes, "adopted various forms of social radicalism."

That Free Methodist Churches were "free" and particularly welcoming to the poor was a social justice expression in and of itself. This intentional and focused hospitality, following biblical precedent and mandate, ran counter to the prevailing trend in urban mainline denominations at the time. What began as outreach became a matter of solidarity; what started as evangelistic fervor developed into distinctive patterns of discipleship, polity, advocacy, leadership style, and organizational ethos. Identity with the poor set the tenor and course for the denomination in profound ways for several generations. The first generation of Free Methodism provides particularly rich examples of living the holy life through doing justice. This is seen in their direct efforts to rectify injustices and establish institutions that would counter or heal social evils, and in writings and speeches intended to convince both Christians and a non-Christian public of the rationality and practicality of biblically-defined justice.

Beyond working to abolish slavery and opting for the poor, Roberts personally involved himself in the Farmers' Alliance, calling farmers to organize in order to influence legislators to repeal high tariffs on items farmers needed and to work to break up the monopolies that controlled prices at farmers' and workers' expense. Free Methodists, though deploring secret societies, made special provision for members to participate in labor unions. They also voted in General Conference to stand against militarism and bore a witness for peace.

Free Methodist schools, colleges, and seminaries were envisioned as models of Christian education that would develop leadership to guide the church and society to reflect more and more God's justice, mercy, and truth. Such institutions would always be accessible to the poor. Many of these primary, secondary, undergraduate, and graduate schools did not survive, but some did — notably Greenville College (IL), Spring Arbor University (MI), Roberts Wesleyan College (NY), Seattle Pacific University (WA), and Central Christian College of Kansas (KS).

Free Methodist commitment to the poor was also expressed in a wide range of mercy- and relief-oriented activities and organizations. Free Methodist works of mercy are discussed in a later chapter, but it is important here to note that the vigorous establishment of rescue missions, clinics and hospitals, orphanages, homes for unwed mothers, outreach to immigrants and other human services — in North America and through world missions — was an outworking of a faith orientation that took the Bible and Wesley's early Methodist principles regarding commitment to love and care for the poor quite seriously.

Roberts tried to influence his own church and the public at large through his writings in *The Earnest Christian* and a series of books written later in life. Of particular note are his efforts to persuade regarding the justice of ordaining women and reforming monetary policy. His little book *First Lessons on Money* (1886) offers insights into the founder's leadership on issues of markets, debt, inheritances, and economic justice. For instance, Roberts disparages mergers and acquisitions for their negative impacts on workers and the market. "Monopolies," he says, "whatever may be their form, operate against the welfare of the community at large." He cautions against undue indebtedness at personal, corporate, and governmental levels. Regarding inherited money, Roberts declares that "our laws should make it difficult for one man to amass a vast fortune and keep it in his family from generation to generation." Regarding influence peddling, he says, "the people should see to it that their representatives in Congress pass laws in *their* interest, and not in favor of the moneyed class and rich corporations to the injury of the community generally." He promotes "systematic benevolence" and quotes the enduring dictum of John Wesley: "Gain all you can, save [conserve] all you can, give all you can."

I don't know how fully doing justice was incorporated into the weekly concerns of Free Methodist members, the practices and preaching of its pastors, and the priorities of its local congregations. But it is difficult to read early conference minutes and books by leaders, or peruse early editions of the *Book of Discipline,* without being aware of a *milieu* in which doing justice was at the center of heart-felt faith and at the forefront of holiness-motivated activities. In numerous instances "doing justice" and "showing mercy" are blended together; for they often go hand in hand. Mercy was not separated from justice, as if one were more or less important than the other or the two were theologically or practically divisible.

### How We Got from There to Here

So, how did we get from *there* to *here*? Most historians link the demise of robust holiness-church focus on doing justice with the Fundamentalist-Modernist controversy. This ecclesiastical conflict has defined ministry at global and local levels for nearly a century. Fundamentalism emerged in the early 1900s in reaction to a growing acceptance among American mainstream churches of German "higher criticism" of the Bible. The theological impact on mainline Protestant churches came to be called Modernism. Over against Modernism, Fundamentalism defended such Christian "fundamentals" as the inerrancy of the Scriptures, virgin birth and deity of Jesus, substitutionary atonement, bodily resurrection of Jesus, and authenticity of Jesus' miracles.

Fundamentalism not only countered liberal theological perspectives, however. It redefined the sole mission of "Bible-believing" churches to be individual soul salvation. Fundamentalism reduced doing justice and social action to a secondary — even unnecessary — place in the theological and ecclesiastical equation. With the rise of Fundamentalism came an environment of polarization and "guilty by association" regarding social justice efforts. Since so-called Modernist churches and organizations believed in and championed social justice efforts, any church or ministry that was involved in social justice advocacy was suspected of "liberalism." In reaction to the negative label "the social gospel," many holiness churches and ministries that earlier promoted social justice and the rights of the poor and oppressed ceased to do so within a generation.

The extent of the impact of the Fundamentalist-Modernist controversy is a subject beyond this presentation. Paul M. Bassett charts the impact of Fundamentalism specifically on holiness churches in articles such as "The Fundamentalist Leavening of the Holiness Movement" as does Stan Ingersol in his chapter in this book.

Fundamentalism, for the good it accomplished, brought with it a suspicion of any church or Christian organization not explicitly focused solely on individual soul salvation, a tendency toward social and political disengagement, and a reduction of social action and outreach to soul-saving charity. Even today, the measure of a so-called "successful" ministry of outreach to the poor or effort for social justice is evaluated primarily by how many conversions it counts. Do church growth experts or holiness leaders evaluate in *the terms Jesus used* when asked about the legitimacy of his ministry? "The blind receive sight, the lame walk, those who have leprosy are cured, the deaf hear, the dead are raised, and the good news is preached to the poor" (Mt. 11:5).

I am convinced that a continuing obstacle to whole-hearted Free Methodist involvement in doing justice is a passive acquiescence to Fundamentalist-based descriptions of salvation. Reticence about the extent to which we should be doing justice is rooted in a deformed view of salvation. We inadvertently buy into a form of metaphysical dualism: souls are for saving; bodies are dispensable. The soul is perfectible; creation is irreparably corrupted. The soul is eternal; substance must pass away. Exclusive focus on singular soul salvation eclipses the real physical, material, social, and structural surroundings in which the soul temporarily lingers.

> Even today, the measure of a "successful" ministry of outreach to the poor or effort for social justice is evaluated primarily by how many conversions it counts.

Do we really believe this? Where is our understanding of the kingdom of God? Does not biblical integrity call on us to address and correct this unbiblical split? Would we not be more faithful to our Wesleyan and holiness heritage to embody ministry expressions and proclamation that refuse to truncate people, divide the gospel message, devalue God's creation and redemptive intention, or sideline the kingdom of God?

The focus on doing justice was not completely lost in the Fundamentalist-Modernist split. Fundamentalism did not leaven the *whole* lump. Evidence shows that Free Methodists did not abandon social justice issues entirely. *The Book of Discipline* witnesses to enduring emphases and new social realities. It indicates that while North American Free Methodists modified some statements as they moved toward a predominantly mainstream, middle-class orientation, they never retracted their historic stands on most social justice issues. The *Disicpline* reveals special care for the spirit and approach to how issues of social injustice are addressed, staying close to early Methodist and holiness roots.

Particularly interesting to me is the firm stand against racial bias that Free Methodists took at the hour of the nation's greatest social crisis of the 20$^{th}$ century. Robert Wall points out that "when conservative Christianity had distanced itself from the civil rights movement ... as being politically liberal, Free Methodists took the remarkable action of affirming the equal worth of all persons and pledged 'a determined effort to eliminate the unchristian practice of racial discrimination and injustice.'"

This 1964 *Book of Discipline* statement against racial bias during the heat of the American civil rights movement is a tribute to faithfulness to our theology and history as well as a mark of leadership. Perhaps this was a turning point or a moment of awakening to reclaim a heritage. Since then, Free Methodists have voted to ordain women and have caringly addressed a widening range of justice concerns. While Free Methodists may not have been as directly engaged in doing justice or in a cutting-edge role as the first generation, more than residual vestiges remain to point to and build on for the future.

**If We are Doing Justice, What Kind of Justice are We Doing?**

Some will argue that today we in fact do justice quite routinely. It is true that much could be made of preventive work against injustice which vigorous inreach and outreach ministries of a local congregation offer. Who can adequately measure the redemptive care and positive spiritual formation impacts that Sunday School, Christian Life Clubs, addictions recovery, Bible study groups, cell groups, counseling, solid biblical preaching, and compassionate outreach achieve in individual, family, congregational, and community lives? Daily and weekly, Free Methodists call people to live as salt and light in the world, equip them to stand against temptation and evil, and form them to be people who are not conformed to the world but who may well transform it. But all our positive, formative, preventive action does not reduce in the least the question of our action or inaction in the face of outright injustice in our community, society, and world.

> Current evangelical issues often overlook or bypass core concerns that originally defined early Free Methodism: poverty, human slavery, and feminism.

Perhaps part of our conversation should focus on *the kind of justice* we Free Methodists are currently prone to do. Obviously over the past twenty-five years Free Methodists have been engaged in the struggle against abortion, the provision of positive alternatives for pregnant women, and other "culture war" issues related to public education, sexuality, bioethics, and court decision-making. On the one hand it appears that "culture war" issues have been framed and promoted completely outside Free Methodism, wed to partisan politics, and accepted by our people. On the other hand it appears that historic concerns of Free Methodists and others have been co-opted and distorted by political influence groups.

In my view, the wedding of partisan-motivated issue advocacy to denominational identity should be resisted at all levels in our ecclesiology and practice, both now and in the future. As we consider involvement in justice issues, we should be asking: Who is initially and ultimately being served by these priorities and passions? Does the manner in which this particular issue is being approached and addressed reflect the Spirit of holiness and our own heritage? And are we thinking globally, or even beyond our own socioeconomic group or consumer desires, when we vote or act?

One more question we should ask: Who is setting the social justice agenda? How are some issues deemed more important than others? Current evangelical issues often overlook and/or bypass core concerns that originally motivated Methodism and defined early Free Methodism: poverty, human slavery, and feminism. Why have poverty and slavery — two of the gravest global issues — hardly registered so far on the agenda of either major American political party? Why are we not alarmed at this? And what might we do in concert with other branches of the body of Christ to focus on these global crises, even if national or Western political will regarding them is currently all but nonexistent?

## Why Free Methodists Should Give More Attention to Doing Justice

Consider four reasons why Free Methodist believers and local congregations should move doing justice toward the center of our lives and practice:

1. Scripture, reason, tradition, and experience — key in early Methodist and Free Methodist heritage — make an unmistakable appeal to us to do justice as core to Free Methodist spiritual formation.

2. The de-formations of Protestant evangelical spirituality under the influence of Fundamentalism and the co-optation of evangelical social justice concern by partisan politics call for a course correction and a reclaiming of biblical and holiness-heritage expressions of doing justice. Can we, with integrity to our history, claim to be Free Methodist or Wesleyan/holiness if we do not move doing justice toward the center of our lives, pastoral leadership, and congregational priorities?

3. The injustice issues at play in a rapidly globalizing economic and international world call for biblically-based, heart-clarifying, and discerningly-sophisticated assessment, advocacy, and action. Poverty is not simply a matter of a lack of local resources or drought or flood. Increasingly it is a matter of global market forces demanding ever-cheaper labor and multinational corporate control (in the name of "democracy" and "free-market economy") over local food supplies, resources, and production. Human trafficking for labor exploitation and the sex trade is as related to market irresponsibilities as is any other issue. The impact of Western consumerism as the highest good is driving the exploitation of children, women, and laborers in ways that begin to mirror 18$^{th}$-century England. And perhaps no theological or ecclesiastical entity connects so closely with poverty and human slavery as Free Methodism.

4. The clarity of Jesus in his announcement of the kingdom of God calls for doing justice as a central part of every disciple's and congregation's life — including a Free Methodist disciple's life and the congregation's life together. Jesus called his followers and the church to *enact* the kingdom's values, practices, and priorities — even in the face of derision, "impracticality," and death — as if the future depended on it.

## The Future Shape of Justice in Free Methodism

Consider the possibilities. What would happen if we made the doing of justice more central made in our lives as Free Methodist believers, pastors, and congregations? What would my weekly devotional life include? As a pastor, what teaching priorities or investments of time do I make? As a congregation, what does our "ministry menu" or thrust of service include? Where do we begin? In the spirit of Wesleyan optimism of grace, consider the shape and indications of a Free Methodism that makes doing justice more central:

*We stop telling ourselves that justice issues are too messy and complicated to get involved in.* We seek to fully understand the nature of particular injustices. We begin to trace their sources in irresponsible or sinful values, actions, approaches, alliances, or habits at personal, corporate, social, and/or national levels.

*We no longer just hope somebody else is doing something about poverty or human trafficking.* We identify how Free Methodists and others are engaging in both relief and redemptive action to counter these injustices. We support this work financially and prayerfully. We identify corrupting activities and also commend best practices to our representative church, government, corporate, and community leaders at all levels.

*We incorporate doing justice into the center of our descriptions and proclamations of salvation and discipleship.* We reclaim biblical guidance regarding doing justice and forge a fresh Free Methodist spiritual formation with this mandate and heritage at heart. We both preach grace and do justice in our evangelism and discipleship. We incorporate "justice, mercy, and truth" into our Christian education, discipleship, leadership development, worship, and group curriculum.

Justice is not something talked about one Sunday of the year; it is woven into the texture of our life together.

*We do not accept at face-value any politically-motivated or fear-based description or solution to social problems or injustices.* We exercise deeper spiritual discernment and a broader sense of social responsibility than can be reduced to sound-bytes, slogans, campaigns, and election-cycle political interest action.

*We are educated and engaged regarding what is being accomplished within the body of Christ regarding historic core Free Methodist concerns* such as poverty, human slavery, and women's issues. We encourage involvement in local and international initiatives like the Christian Community Development Association, the Blueprint to End Homelessness, and the International Justice Mission.

*We take a global approach to doing justice.* We move beyond Americanism — for the sake of authentic Christianity and our brothers and sisters in Christ around the world. We address specifically American justice challenges like homelessness, affordable housing, livable wages, affordable health care, and access to quality public education at all levels, within a global perspective. North American and Western lifestyles and choices are linked with the prevention or propagation of global poverty, human trafficking, fair labor, women's rights, and economic domination.

*We openly commit to solidarity with the poor and the plight of the poorest of the poor in our society and globally.* As best we can, we look at the world through the eyes of marginalized people and groups. Instead of insulating ourselves from contact with the poor, we look for ways to engage the poor with meaning, linking our own lives inseparably with theirs. We visit, develop relationships, and become increasingly aware of the immediate struggles of neighbors. We give more weight to their testimonies and experiences than to politicians and news media sources. We work with neighbors to understand and address poverty.

*As we act for relief of the poor and vulnerable, we link relief with reform and establish just structures, policies, and opportunities whenever possible.* As we give ourselves to salvage lives that have been swept over the proverbial waterfall, we just as readily move expediently to address what has caused people and groups to be swept downstream in the first place. We treat symptoms and we address sources. To expand a well-worn adage: Give people fish, teach them how to fish, guarantee their right to fish, and do all in your power to insure that the water upstream is not being polluted, so they can actually eat and sell the fish they catch.

*We are as redemptively involved in our communities for social reform as we are in our congregations for spiritual formation and revival.* Free Methodist spiritual formation encourages active neighboring as well as service to support congregational life. Volunteers serve local justice concerns in balance with congregational outreach ministries. We see the two as complementary, not competitive or exclusionary.

*We act as responsible investors in the global market.* If we invest in the stock market or benefit from stock market investments (such as through tax-sheltered retirement accounts), we do so, as much as possible, without blindly contributing to or benefiting from unjust labor or unethical business practices. We refrain from investments that promote violence, war-making, addictions, or unfair trade and labor practices. We examine local labor and market practices of companies in which we invest and call for social responsibility. When stock-market and multinational corporate activity is identified as rapacious, we call for accountability and change.

*We act as responsible consumers of global products, resources, and services.* We see a higher value than the lowest price tag. We challenge our habits of purchasing and consuming whenever we discover they directly or indirectly feed injustices for laborers and the poor around the world.

*We refute violence against human beings in all its forms.* We speak prophetically to militarism and the violence of unjust war — and we also reject the language and norms of violence in our society and world. Instead we engage in, pursue, and encourage ways of conflict resolution and *shalom*-bearing that give positive testimony to the power of a holy God whose way is love.

*We address justice issues in the Spirit and manner of perfect love.* As we identify injustice, seek to relieve the oppressed, call perpetrators of injustice to accountability, and work for reform, we do so with the redemption of the perpetrating individual or organization in focus. Our very approach and spirit is the key to transformative outcomes. One early Free Methodist put it this way: "To find the remedy is easy; successfully to apply it involves the principle of holiness."

*We show by example and precedent what is possible when people of heart-felt faith and vision creatively engage the call to do justice.* We demonstrate the promise of restorative justice initiatives. We model best practices in socially redemptive ministries and volunteer services. We are proactive instead of reactive. To the best of our ability and acting with all the light that we collectively have, we exemplify to the best of our ability the principles of the kingdom of God.

We live earnestly the petition we constantly make: "Your kingdom come, Your will be done on earth as it is in heaven."

## Bibliography of Sources

Bakke, Ray. *The Urban Christian.* Downer's Grove, Illinois: InterVarsity Press, 1987.

Conn, Harvie. *A Clarified Vision for Urban Mission.* Grand Rapids, Michigan: Zondervan Publishing House, 1987.

———. *Evangelism: Preaching Grace and Doing Justice.* Grand Rapids, Michigan: Zondervan Publishing House, 1982.

Dayton, Donald. *Discovering an Evangelical Heritage.* New York: Harper & Row, 1976.

———. "The Holiness Churches: A Significant Ethical Tradition" *The Christian Century,* (Feb. 26, 1975): 197-201.

Edgar, James. *Reconnecting the Urban Neighborhood Church.* Columbus, Ohio: The Methodist Board of Mission, 1988.

Hauerwas, Stanley & William Willimon. *Resident Aliens.* Nashville: Abingdon, 1990.

Hynson, Leon O. "The Social Concerns of Wesley: Theological Foundations." *Christian Scholar's Review* (Vol. 4, No. 1, 1974): 36-51.

Jennings, Theodore W. Jr. *Good News to the Poor: John Wesley's Evangelical Economics.* Nashville: Abingdon, 1990.

Niebuhr, H. Richard. *Christ and Culture.* New York: Harper & Row, 1951.

Palmer, Parker. *The Active Life: A Spirituality of Work, Creativity, and Caring.* San Francisco: Harper & Row, 1990.

Payne, Ruby K. *Poverty: A Framework for Understanding and Working with Students and Adults from Poverty.* Baytown, Texas: RFT Publishing, 1995.

Pohl, Christine. *Making Room: Recovering Hospitality as a Christian Tradition.* Grand Rapids: Eerdmans, 2000.

Runyon, Theodore, ed. *Sanctification & Liberation.* Nashville: Abingdon, 1981.

Smith, Timothy L. *Revivalism and Social Reform.* Nashville: Abingdon, 1957.

Stone, Bryan P. *Compassionate Ministry: Theological Foundations.* Maryknoll, New York: Orbis Books, 1996.

Stringfellow, William. *A Private and Public Faith.* Grand Rapids: Eerdmans, 1962.

Thompson, Marjorie J. "To Do Justice," *Weavings,* (Vol. 1, No. 2, November/December, 1986): 22-29.

Tracy, Wesley D. "The Wesleyan Way to Spiritual Formation." San Francisco: An unpublished doctoral dissertation at the Theological Seminary of San Francisco.

Truesdale, Albert L., Steve Weber, eds. *Evangelism and Social Redemption.* Kansas City: Nazarene Publishing House, 1987.

Willard, Dallas. *Spirit of the Disciplines.* San Francisco: Harper & Row, 1988.

Wink, Walter. *Engaging the Powers.* Minneapolis: Fortress Press, 1992.

Winter, Gibson. *Suburban Captivity of the Churches.* New York: Macmillan, 1962.

Yoder, John H. *The Politics of Jesus.* Grand Rapids: Eerdmans, 1972.

## CHAPTER 7
# *Free Methodist Mission: Mercy*

Henry G. Church
Pastor, former Area Director for Africa
Free Methodist World Missions

The Free Methodist soul is a nebulous thing, hard to find, and when you find it, hard to grasp firmly. In an attempt to grasp it firmly enough to dissect it in search of *mercy*, I thought it would help to try to define the terms "mercy" and "soul." I found them as difficult to pin down as the Free Methodist soul itself.

Mercy is defined as "pity, bowels of compassion, tenderheartedness, compassion, forgiving, benevolent, mild."[1] Samuel Fallows describes it as "kind acts proceeding from inward compassion. A desire to relieve such as are in misery and want."[2]

Mercy has been described as "That compassion which causes one to help the weak, the sick, or the poor. Showing mercy is one of the cardinal virtues of a true Christian (James 2:1-13), and is one of the determinants of God's treatment to us. Christian mercy is a part of the fruit of the Spirit made up in part of love, longsuffering, gentleness and goodness."[3]

"Soul" is even more difficult. There are Hebrew and Greek words that define it, of course, but most of us are not readily acquainted with the subtle nuances one finds there. To even try to explain them in English causes them to lose sharp definition.

The *Popular and Critical Bible Encyclopaedia and Scriptural Dictionary* seems to define it fairly well: Soul is "not only the entire inner nature of man but also his personality. . . . It is that vital active principle in man, which perceives, remembers, reasons, loves, hopes, fears, compares, desires, resolves, adores, imagines, and aspires after immortality." This work translates the Greek word for "soul" as "the simple meaning of 'life.'"[4]

Mercy, then, is an issue of the soul as people's inner nature, that vital active principle which gives us life, that animating factor that motivates compassion to help the weak and the sick and the needy. Mercy must issue from somewhere. Even the ungodly have a soul and are capable of mercy. Every person has a touch of the image of God within the soul that enables them to respond to situations in mercy.

But for the Christian, somehow mercy must issue from a soul that is not only animated physically but quickened spiritually so that it can give forth the fruits of what God expects in a God-centered life — love, longsuffering, gentleness and goodness.

What about the Free Methodist soul? Where does mercy come from among Free Methodists? If the soul is the source of animation, life, vitality, then that is what we need to look for, and how it expresses itself in acts of mercy among Free Methodists.

David McKenna in *A Future with a History* describes the waning of the soul as the weakening of the pulse or heartbeat. He suggests that the pulse was very faint at the end of the first century of the church, in 1960. Yet today the beat does go on.[5] We know it does, or there would be no vitality in any of the church's activities of this generation. In the Foreword to McKenna's book, John Van Valin asserts, "The Free Methodist Church again seeks to define its soul, articulate its mission, respond to its origin, and seek a fresh understanding of God's purpose for this day."[6] That is what I do here, examining how this soul is expressing itself in mercy.

## A Tradition of Mercy

Mercy is in the DNA of true Free Methodists. McKenna mentions mercy and mercy-related attitudes at least seventeen times in his book. B.T. Roberts, our principal founder, was known to often divide his wardrobe with the frontier preacher whose coat had grown "seedy" and thin with age. His attitude toward the young preachers in their ministries was one of merciful guidance and encouragement.[7] He was a man of mercy.

Bishop L.R. Marston notes in his centennial history of the Free Methodist Church that in the early days of the denomination (1885) Gerry Homes was set up to care for the aged and to children needing institutional care. In 1886 another home was started in Woodstock, Illinois. In 1888, the founder of Woodstock incorporated Chicago Industrial Home for Children. In 1907 the Light and Life Children's Home of Kansas City was founded, developing out of city mission work, to find homes for babies that needed adopting. The Children's Home cared for over five thousand children in their first fifty-two years.

Deaconess Hospital was organized in Oklahoma City, beginning as a rescue home for unfortunate girls in 1900. For years it carried the name "Home of Redeeming Love" for its program for girls in trouble. Talk about merciful! Another one hundred or more children were cared for by the Jolley Home in Conyers, Georgia, founded in 1947.[8] The primary motivation of these ministries was mercy, compassion and evangelism.

These ministries became institutions and no longer exist in their early form. If the Free Methodist Church in this generation is to find ways for mercy to issue from its soul, it must look for new paradigms.

World missions is another area where mercy overflowed from the Free Methodist soul. As early as 1881 Free Methodists were going to the far-flung areas of the world, with or without general church support. They were called to tell the love of Jesus to the lost of the world and to show his mercy as they met the needs of lost people through evangelism, education, medical care and leadership training. From 1920 to 1995, 105 missionaries served twenty-five years or more.[9] Today however the average mission career is seven years. In the decade between 1960 and 1970 the average number of FM missionaries in Africa was well over one hundred, with 130 or more having served during that period. Today, we have ten career missionaries in Africa. At one time the peak number of FM missionaries on the field worldwide was over 260. Today it is less than one hundred. Thankfully, that decline has now stopped and a reversal of the trend has begun.

Free Methodist missions were very active in starting

schools, opening clinics and hospitals, training health-care workers, planting churches, and generally reaching out to the poor. The reason for doing these things was, first, a response to specific calls from God and, secondly, *mercy* flowing from their Free Methodist souls, needing an outlet. They found it in the needy of the world.

**Mercy in World Missions Today**

When you look at some statistics, you can get discouraged. The decline of FM missionaries in Africa from over a hundred to ten missionaries can look discouraging, for example. But look at the larger picture. In 1980 there were about 90,000 Free Methodists outside North America, 55,000 of these in Africa. Today we count more than a half million in Africa! In 1980 Free Methodist missionaries served in seven countries on the African continent. Today we are in twenty-five, plus some unpublicized "creative access" areas. And we have new churches in Iraq and Jordan. We are finding new ways of extending mercy to the world.

One of the tragedies of today's world is masses of children in need. Many thousands of HIV/AIDS-affected families are found in Africa and other places. Pastors and leaders in undeveloped areas need a helping hand. They cry out for mercy.

International Child Care Ministries has come alongside to provide education, medical care, clothing, food, and other help for hundreds of these children. Nearly 13,500 sponsors now reach out in mercy to over 20,000 kids in thirty countries of the world.[10]

In the days just before writing this paper, I visited a remote rural village in northern Malawi — a small trading center called Tukombo. The local Free Methodist church serves that village and reaches out with seven or eight additional preaching points. The pastor is Leonard Banda, who also serves as superintendent of the Northern Conference. The purpose of our visit was to see what his village was doing for HIV/AIDS-affected children.

The Free Methodist HIV/AIDS program in this village began in 1993. People in the church saw that the children needed food, clothing, school supplies, and other things. They believed the Scripture from James 1:27 and 1 Timothy 5 and knew they must have mercy on these needy kids. Pastor Banda did not come to the mission for assistance, nor to any non-government organization (NGO). He and his people rallied around those kids and began to help them directly. They hired themselves out to neighbors and business people to plow and plant for others so they could earn money to take care of the kids.

The church started a garden that now raises food for these kids. These Free Methodists have expanded the effort to help needy kids in the community who are outside the church. Today fifty children from three to sixteen years of age are being helped. The church also provides Bible lessons and AIDS counseling as they can.

I saw the kids. They are healthy and happy. Someone had mercy on them.

These are stories of the compassion side of mercy. "Blessed are the merciful, for they will be shown mercy," Jesus said (Mt. 5:7). We must reach out in merciful compassion if we are going to rediscover our soul.

> We must reach out in merciful compassion if we are to rediscover our soul.

Even more importantly: God's gracious forgiving mercy is what we really are all about. We are nothing more than a humanitarian organization if all we do is minister to the orphan and give Child Care money to help kids. It is merciful and it is a part of our heritage to care for the poor. But without the extension of the forgiving mercy of God, this is all wasted effort. Jesus asked what profit it would be if we gained the whole world but lost our soul.

Where is the Free Methodist soul in this area of extending God's mercy?

I cannot speak with much authority about the church in the West; I have been living in another culture too long. When I come to the U.S. for brief periods, I am often shocked at what the church has become. While we have "open arms" and a good philosophy and our theology is basically correct, the

Western church seems to have gone very far from its roots. When we get too far away, I don't know how our soul survives. It seems to me in many ways the Western church has let the "world press us into its mold" in spite of the Apostle Paul's warning in Romans 12. I do not know if the soul of the American Free Methodist Church has survived and if mercy still flows from it as it did long ago.

But, I can answer for Africa!

**Stories from Africa**

Brother Nasiyaya still serves the Lord with a joyful heart and a glad countenance. I saw him two weeks ago. I also saw him when he was a new Christian, in 1998. I was doing my Ph.D. research in village churches in Malawi. I interviewed Nasiyaya to see why he was a Free Methodist. He was more interested in telling me a story.

Mr. Nasiyaya and his family were hungry. They had no food in the village. He went to visit Pastor Chimombo. While Nasiyaya was visiting in the pastor's house, Chimombo was called outside to meet with someone else. Nasiyaya looked around and saw three bags of dry beans (50 kilograms each). He saw that no one else was in the house. He looked, and the pastor could not see in the door.

Nasiyaya moved near the bags and began to fill his pockets with beans. When they were full, he sidled out and waved at the pastor and said the equivalent of "See you later."

"That night," he said, "we ate beans for dinner. But my stomach did not feel too well. The beans didn't sit in the right place." He couldn't sleep. The next day they had beans again, and again he didn't feel right.

On the third day, Nasiyaya went to the pastor and said, "Pastor, I have sinned. I stole your beans. I want to pay them back by working for you. I have no money to pay you. Please forgive me." He told me, with a smile too big for his face, "The pastor forgave me. God forgave me. I will never steal beans again!"

Mercy! The mercy of God who would not let him go until he made things right. That is basic holiness! Nasiyaya knows, and I saw it.

Another story: It was a very dark night. We were sitting in a circle around a fire. We were in the Zimbabwe bush, miles from so-called civilization. An old-fashioned District Quarterly Meeting was being held in the village of a Free Methodist evangelist, Mapapeni by name.

We had eaten and now the golden firelight reflected from the dark faces of the Christians around the flames. It was a dramatic moment as different ones shared their testimony. The evening was coming to a close and we all stood around the fire. We held hands in a circle and began singing the Shangaan version of "There is Power in the Blood."

Suddenly the tranquil beauty of the moment was shattered as to my right, just two or three persons away, a young woman shrieked and tried to pull loose from the circle and run away. She was possessed by an evil spirit. Immediately Mapapeni, who was on one side of her, and the person on the other grabbed her. Soon she was on her back on the ground.

One person was holding each arm. Mapapeni had his hands on her head and was praying in a very loud voice, "*Huma! Huma!* Come out! Come out!" The rest of us continued holding hands around the fire and singing, "There is power, power, wonder-working power, in the precious blood of the Lamb."

Several minutes later the young woman was delivered from the evil spirit. She stood to her feet and rejoined the circle, holding hands and singing with us, "There is wonder-working power in the blood."

That is mercy! God's mercy. The church was the tool God used to apply his mercy to the beaten and bound heart and set it free.

Here's another story. Langbuoy was completing his final classes at the Malawi Bible School. As was the custom, he was given a chapel period to address the students on any topic he wished. These were always interesting sessions because you never knew what was coming.

Langbuoy was no exception. When he began his address he simply said he wanted to give his testimony. None of us was ready for what he had to say.

Langbuoy Banda began attending the Free Methodist Church near his home because he liked to sing in the choir and enjoyed the fellowship. Recognizing Langbuoy's innate leadership skills, his pastor suggested he attend Bible school and train for ministry. So he applied, was accepted, and began attending classes.

No one knew about his girlfriend, not even his wife. This relationship continued for a couple of years while Banda was in school. The school consists of three intensive month-long modules each year for five years, so there was plenty of time between modules to see his girl friend and spend time with his family.

Langbuoy told the students, "One night we had a very unusual chapel service. Rev. Church made a cross from two pieces of firewood and built a fire nearby. He had little papers and nails and hammers and pencils. During chapel he told us that if we had a sin in our life, or a big temptation, or had left troubles at home when we came to school, or any other problem, we were free to write this problem on a paper and nail it to the cross. He promised that no one would see the papers but the writer and God. So my friends went to the fireside and wrote what they felt on the paper. But there was no way I was going to write *my* sin on that paper! I just scribbled on the paper and nailed it to the cross. Nothing changed in my life."

Langbuoy went on. "A year later — I don't know why he did it, but Rev. Church did that same chapel service again. That time, as I sat and watched the fire, I thought about it. I wondered, 'Can God forgive *my* sin?' That night I wrote my sin on the paper and nailed it to the cross. As Rev. Church and the other teacher put the cross on the fire, I saw the flames take my paper and I saw the smoke lift toward heaven, and I knew I was forgiven. I went home and told the girl to get lost. I told my wife what I had been doing and promised it would never happen again, and it hasn't. God has called me to be a preacher and I am going to serve him!"

Today Langbuoy Banda is in Mozambique. He is the first African missionary sent by a Southern Africa conference to cross a border and plant churches. He is successful and happy, and redeemed. Mercy! Probably the mercy of God kept him from getting AIDS. The mercy of God changed his life so radically he can never be the same. The Free Methodist Church has not lost its soul in Africa — not yet!

Then there's Julius, who used to work in the mines in South Africa. He went back home when his contract was finished. The pastor of the Blantyre, Malawi, Free Methodist Church met him and led him to the Lord.

I went to Malawi on a visit. We were living in Zimbabwe at the time. When I stopped to visit that pastor, Julius was on the pastor's porch, visiting. After greetings and proper introductions the pastor explained, "This is Julius. You wouldn't have wanted to meet him before he was a Christian. He used to hide in dark places and beat people and take their money. He was a bad man." Then he said with a twinkle in his eye, "But now he is different. Jesus has changed his life."

We spent a nice afternoon and evening in conversations. It grew late and time for bed. The pastor said, "Before we go to bed we want to go into the house and have prayers, if that is OK." Well, of course it was OK! Julius and I sat in chairs the pastor had provided while we waited for the family and neighbors to join us. About thirty little children followed us in and sat along one wall in the small ten-by-ten-foot room. Of course they acted like children, poking, hitting, complaining, just being normal.

As the noise level rose, Julius stood and walked to the children. It suddenly got quiet. I wondered what he would do.

He bent over the boys and girls and asked, "Do you know this song?" and he began to sing. "*Yesu, ndi wa bwino. Yesu, ndi wa bwino, ndi wa bwino kwambiri.* Jesus is so good. Jesus is so good. He is so good to me."

The children joined in joyfully and I sat and watched with tears in my eyes. A guy you wouldn't want to meet because he was so mean! Now, so gentle he could lead children in singing, God is so good to me. Mercy! There is no other reason why Julius should be saved. He was not good enough. He was bad! But God had mercy and used the church to carry it to Julius.

**Mercy in Jesus' Cross**

Paul said to the Corinthians, "The message of the cross is foolishness to those who are perishing, but to us who are being saved it is the power of God" (1 Cor. 1:18). There is power in the message of the cross. That message is MERCY! There is mercy for all. This mercy is free. God sits on the Mercy Seat. There is plenty. This is the message that is foolishness to the perishing but power to the believer.

From the soul of the church comes the gospel of life-changing mercy and pardon, cleaning and cleansing. As long as *that* message is preached, the church will not lose its soul.

Where I live, the Free Methodist soul is alive and you don't have to search for it. It is obvious by the mercy.

**Endnotes**
[1] James Hastings, ed., *Dictionary of the Bible,* Vol. III (New York/ Edinburgh: Charles Scribner, 1900), 345-46.
[2] Samuel Fallows, ed., *The Popular and Critical Bible Encyclopaedia and Scriptural Dictionary* (Howard Severance Co., 1922), 1144.
[3] Merrill C. Tenney, ed., *Zondervan Pictorial Dictionary* (Grand Rapids: Zondervan, 1963), 525.
[4] Fallows, 1606.
[5] David McKenna, *A Future with a History* (Light and Life Communications, 1997), 186.
[6] Van Valin in McKenna, ix.
[7] Clarence H. Zahniser, *Earnest Christian: Life and Works of Benjamin Titus Roberts* (Advocate Publishing House, 1957), 181.
[8] Leslie R. Marston, *From Age to Age A Living Witness* (Light and Life Press, 1960), 441-45.
[9] McKenna, 363-68 (with names listed).
[10] Statistics from Ann Van Valin, Director of International Child Care Ministries, a ministry of Free Methodist World Missions, February 15, 2006.

## CHAPTER 8
# Free Methodist Mission: Truth

U. Milo Kaufmann
Author and Poet, English Faculty (retired),
University of Illinois, Urbana-Champaign

My professional life has been spent working on the campus of a secular research university, so I am acutely aware that at least three distinct understandings of truth are current in our culture.

I can illustrate by pointing to the Noyes Chemistry Building on the main quad of my university. In that building for years I taught the literature of fantasy to a large annual congregation of undergraduates from every college on campus.

There is heavy irony for me in the fact that forty years earlier, two uncles of mine, trained at Houghton and Oberlin, studied for their Ph.D.s in chemistry at my school, no doubt using the same building. Those two uncles, part of a family of twelve siblings, were, to my knowledge lost to faith and the church. The truth of science displaced the truth of Christian faith.

That still other truth — of literature and the arts — is well captured in the fantasies of hope and imagination (for example) that I was happy to teach.

So here are three often competing understandings of truth: The truth of science, the truth of literature, and the truth of the Christian faith.

The Christian faith is symbolized by the various university foundations that ring the central campus where I taught. These bridges between area churches and the campus represent an institution that was in fact created by the Methodists of Urbana many years ago. They witness to the truth of special revelation.

I lament the fact that these three sorts of truth are so regularly segregated in our culture. The religious purchase on truth has much to learn from the rigor of science, as well as from the imaginative and often hopeful expansiveness of literature and the arts. The approach of science can help us to be honest about the actual, while the approach of the arts can keep us aware of the boundless expanse of the possible.

**Three Lenses:**
**The Naive Observer, the Partisan, and the Ironic Partisan**

As we consider truth and our Free Methodist tradition, I begin with several miscellaneous comments using three carefully defined stances: Those of the naive observer, the partisan, and the ironic partisan. First however I offer a capsule statement. Think of it as a time-release capsule, for its sense is condensed enough to ask for an extended period of what I hope is useful consideration.

Historically defined, we Free Methodists are a branch of the church committed to both a confident supernaturalism and a radical empiricism. With respect to the first, we part company with the secular world and with much of the more liberal part of the Protestant constituency. With respect to the second, which implies looking always to actual experience, we are in the grand tradition of Wesleyanism, of American revivalism as epitomized in Jonathan Edwards and others, and also of American pragmatism as exemplified by William James (who incidentally was used approvingly by Bishop L.R. Marston in his centennial Free Methodist history).

> **Historically, Free Methodists have been committed both to a confident supernaturalism and a radical empiricism, both revelation and experience.**

But radical empiricism always has difficulty with finding exact and unambiguous language for speaking of religious experience. That difficulty with language is most apparent, naturally, if a particular experience is infrequent. We are wise to keep track of our terminology, always checking it against the lived and the actual.

The responsible and creative uses of language have been my professional concerns. Language ought to be precise, and when it cannot be precise, it must be evocative of the complex, even paradoxical truth of any experience referenced. Often, language best serves the truth when it tells stories, which may well be the testimony of the primary experiencers.

Language can pull away from effective evocation, no longer truly communicating experience. The proof-stories may become had to find the witness of one age has not been well carried over to the next. A radical empiricism is honest as to the real state of affairs. It is unsolicited objective reporting. It is a phenomenology. On the other hand — and I stress this — confident supernaturalism is at ease with reports of the miraculous, the heavenly, the perfect, the gracious, the impossible but true. A robust supernaturalism, lived out, will mean that a radical empiricism taps into stories of the humanly impossible, and yet true. In our tradition supernaturalism finds specific expression in our hope-filled beliefs about the sundry works of the Holy Spirit, about Providence, and about the promised future. If, however, a conspicuous gap opens up between supernaturalist belief and actual practice — if the disciplines which foster the regular manifestation of the miraculous wither away, if familiar terms cease to have any meaningful reference — then we have the rule and reign of irony.

Now that was quite a capsule, but I assure you it can be downed more readily than getting a pill down the throat of any cat I have ever known.

Now for a definition of three different stances vis-à-vis the truth of our tradition. The first of these, that of *the naive observer*, is the non-insider or newcomer. He or she has access to appearances, to public information, to numbers, to printed material, to what some would call the objective and others the superficial, but which I am inclined to call the "aspect," or the face of the matter.

Here's an example of the naive observer. Recently a newcomer appeared at our Champaign-Urbana congregation. Our church building is just fourteen years old. To us old-timers it is still new, but the newcomer sees it differently. To this naive observer the church building looks tired. The carpets are spotted, kitchen tiles need replacing, a clutter of things fill the corners. Do we have a plan, this observer wonders.

The second stance is that of *the partisan*. This is the committed insider. The Free Methodist partisan typically has relatives in the church. A father or grandfather perhaps was a preacher. The partisan has some familiarity or connection with Indianapolis. If asked, he or she probably could find Winona Lake on a map.

Then there is, thirdly, *the ironic partisan*. Such a person is a loyal critic, active in pointing out ironies, especially those discrepancies between profession and practice. The ironic partisan, because he or she is a partisan, is also committed to resolving the ironies. A good example was Charles Kingsley. I worked with Brother Kingsley on his autobiography, helping him cut it by half so it wouldn't be longer than the Bible, and working on emphasis so his lifelong skirmishing with his beloved church would feature solutions rather than problems. Charles was always impatient with a church that considered itself evangelical but did precious little real evangelizing.

Now what would the naive observer, the partisan, and the ironic partisan tell us about *truth* as we affirm it in the Free Methodist community?

**The Naive Observer**

The naive observer would, I think, notice the following truths about the Free Methodist Church in the United States:

1. Numberwise the church has been in a protracted decline in the United States, even as global membership has mushroomed. In 1925 there were 1,284 Free Methodist churches with 80,000 in Sunday school and about 40,000 members. The Church of the Nazarene, almost half a century later than the Free Methodist denomination, had 1,500 churches in 1925, with 60,000 communicants.

In 2002, Free Methodist figures showed 852 churches with 73,000 members, while the Church of the Nazarene counted 5,000 churches and 644,000 members. The Nazarenes showed a 1,000 percent increase while the Free Methodist Church, in number of churches and in membership as a percentage of the U. S. total population, showed sharp decline.

The naive observer looking only at the United States

would say the movement is a spent force. Of course we praise God for our extraordinary constituency in Africa and substantial growth elsewhere in the world.

2. In giving, Free Methodists continue to be generous, but the distribution of giving over the decades has shifted. Between 1968 and 2003 giving as a percentage of per capita disposable income dropped from 9.6 percent to 7.6 percent — still a respectable figure, given the fact that according to David Barrett, Christian giving globally is only 2.26 percent of income.

The fraction of Free Methodist giving that went for benevolence dropped by half in this period. The Church of the Nazarene over the same period saw a drop in giving from 6.5 percent to 4.2 percent, but the decline in benevolence as a percentage of the whole was only a third. Without thorough inspection, a straightforward interpretation of the data is that we Free Methodists, while generous, are not as generous as we once were. Assuming some relationship between love and money, we are not funding our love as we once did.

3. In our language for our signal teaching about the deeper life made possible through the work of God the Holy Spirit, we demonstrate what to a philologist must appear as a checkered and puzzling history.

I have been working with six histories of the Free Methodist Church, as well as with a very modest survey of living witnesses. In John McGeary's 1908 history we encounter the language of "worldliness," "formalism," "Zinzendorfism," and "gradualism." If you hadn't guessed, all of these are bad. McGeary gives high honor to the phrase "entire sanctification."

Bishop Marston's history published in 1960 does not index the term "worldliness," and Marston was himself very much a man of the world in the positive sense, having made a reputation as a child psychologist before becoming a paid churchman. He discusses "formalism" wisely, contrasting it with "fanaticism," but making use of William James and recognizing a spectrum rather than just the two poles. Curiously, Marston has six index listings for sanctification and five for "perfect love," but no listing for "entire sanctification."

David McKenna, in his fine history of recent decades published in 1997, has one index listing for "formalism," but none for "worldliness" and none for "perfect love" or "perfection." He does have thirty references for "entire sanctification."

In the pose of naive observer, but one who has eavesdropped on many, many sermons over six decades, I would note that the language of worldliness and perfection has dropped out altogether from our discourse, along with "Zinzendorfism" and "gradualism." The first of this second pair, by the way, is the position that sanctification is part of regeneration. "Gradualism" affirms a lifelong process of sanctification. "Formalism" is plainly at the exit door. "Entire sanctification" has retained some currency in recent decades, though I rarely hear it used now.

As a denomination we have established something like détente with the world and worldliness, and with formalism and forms in worship. We are reluctant to speak of perfection in a culture awash with insights of biology and depth psychology, and yet we still see merit in believing, if not very effectively teaching, the truth of a post-regeneration crisis in the believer's experience of God the Holy Spirit. Biological insight makes us uneasy talking any more about "eradication," "extirpation," "carnality," "the old man," or "inbred sin." I have not heard any of those terms used homiletically in at least two decades. But then I have missed a few of the sermons preached in that time.

One hundred years after the founding of the Free Methodist Church, the 1960 *Book of Discipline* adjusted somewhat the language about the sinful nature. Bear in mind that if we choose to speak at all about sinful "nature," those secular thinkers who make "nature" their inclusive focus will have things to contribute to the discussion.

I served on the doctoral committee of a very capable woman who has since published perhaps a dozen books. Her thesis on Nathaniel Hawthorne touched on the phenomenon of 19th-century perfectionism. I have gone back to that dissertation recently. She was right, I think, to give a historical context in this country for perfectionist thought and language. I believe it still important and possible to teach a crisis work of sanctification, but the language of "perfection" is very difficult to use. I recall Dr. Mary Tenney's embarrassment when Elton Trueblood, the great Quaker scholar and theologian, asked her point blank, "And you, Miss Tenney. Would you say that you have been perfected in love?"

Still in the pose of naive observer I conducted an amateurish survey of seven adult Christians in my home church, and seven more on the staff at the World Ministry Center in Indianapolis. The results are suggestive, if not conclusive. I asked just three questions, and for each question there were only three permissible answers: Yes, No, and "I prefer not to answer without further definition of terms." The three questions were (1) Have you been entirely sanctified; (2) Have you been perfected in love for God and other persons; and (3) Have you, in a single crisis work of the Holy Spirit in your heart, been delivered from the inclination to sin?

The results were surprising to me in more than one way. Of the fourteen, seven allowed as Yes, they had been entirely sanctified. Yet only two of the fourteen claimed to have been perfected in love for God and other persons. J.A. Wood, writing in 1906 on the subject of perfect love, insisted that "perfect love, perfection, sanctification, holiness" are utterly synonymous. But our several respondents clearly saw that different clusters of meanings are implied. I would say that they are anything but synonymous, though they may be strongly associated.

On the matter of once-and-for-all deliverance from sinful inclination, seven in my survey said Yes, but one of the respondents, a psychiatrist, cheated by adding to his Yes, the phrase "more than once."

To sum up these comments of the naive observer: The numbers for the Free Methodist Church in the U.S. are indicative of a least a tired church, if not a declining one. The usages of the language for the deeper life are indicative of historic change, of communication-overload, and so, I gather, only modest reproduction of the defining experience. We would need many oral histories gathered in the next several years to assess appropriately the wisdom and truth of our historic witness.

## The Partisan

The partisan, stressing the core truths of Free Methodist faith, would I believe point to eight convictions. But before listing those eight, I make a bold claim about how we have behaved ourselves theologically.

With its emphasis upon experience, Wesleyan theology has typically avoided two reductions to absurdity. These are the absurdities that follow from a "hyperlogical" theology, one which refuses to rest in antinomy or yoked contraries. The principal antinomy, of course, is that between fate and freedom. An extreme development of God's will as fate ends with a god far worse than the devil. I have often said I would be a happy atheist before I accepted any version of god which makes him the creator of millions of persons he intends to damn to perpetual torment.

At the other extreme is the humanism which makes persons utterly free. As the Puritan Richard Sibbes once observed, if a person is perfectly free, then he is God.

So let us rest with the paradox of fate and freedom, avoiding the absurdities of a god worse than Satan, and of humans equal to God. We might be wise, as well, to trust antinomy a bit more in speaking of perfection and sinful nature — as Wesley himself does implicitly in his magnificent text for the covenant service printed in our hymnal, and as the collect does in the communion service we celebrate, and as we find in the actual testimony of sanctified persons.

Our *Book of Discipline* from 1860 forward, in the article on entire sanctification, has without embarrassment embraced the antinomy of further spiritual growth after the crisis of sanctification. That sounds like gradualism, but a sanctified gradualism.

Now to eight core truths of Free Methodist faith. (I do not pretend to be exhaustive.) These are the ways we understand truth.

1. *We accept transcendence*, which is to say the supernatural and the miraculous. Nature is far from being all that is.

2. *God's will and Word are to be submitted to*. We approach Scripture as authoritative, expecting that God will address us with conviction, instruction, and encouragement. In my

graduate training in language and literature I was schooled to be critical of texts. But in the case of Scripture, I find that the text is marvelously critical of me, but not only critical. It is also life-defining and enhancing. God as Spirit does indwell His Word.

3.  *The resurrected Jesus Christ is very much alive* and makes himself known to us in the communion of spirit with Spirit. Christian assurance is just one of the evidences of our intimate relationship with a living Christ.

4.  *The fundamental disciplines of the Christian life are regular Bible-reading and prayer.*

5.  *God's great invention, after the world, is the church.* This unique fellowship of the forgiven and the inquiring has no earthly equivalent, and is the "antepast [foretaste] of Heaven." (Sermon-tract, "I Believe in the Church", Lloyd Knox, out of print.)

6.  *Because God loves us each one, utterly, without regard to our merit or works, we are freed to be concerned about persons other than ourselves.*

7.  Unlike the way things are with some fatalistic theologies, *we believe that there is such a thing as Christian growth.* The twelve-year-old Jesus, after all, could increase in favor with God and man. That conundrum is of a piece with the insistence that salvation is a thing to be worked out lifelong. No crisis of grace should end in antinomianism or inertness.

8.  *We have a message of the best news imaginable,* a message to be shared with the world. God is reconciled. If you are not already so reconciled, BE reconciled to God. Every good thing is promised to those who believe, world without end, forever and ever.

You will notice that these eight convictions do not really constitute what Bishop Marston, coining a term, called "distinctives." They do not so much set us off from all other Christians as put us squarely in the grand tradition. I can rest with defining differences — "soul-marks," if you like — which involve church polity, geography, ethnic history, or habits of worship. I am much less comfortable with an identify founded upon claims of uniquely-privileged theological discernment.

Historian McGeary could claim that it is only as Free Methodists live by "peculiar doctrines" that they are faithful to the church's mission. That seems to me to be too much the language of religious war rather than of effective witness and evangelism. I recall the cliché that the first casualty of war is the truth.

In my youth I did hear claims about Scriptural holiness which implied, on a par with statements of the most hardnosed supralapsarian Calvinist, that the vast majority of persons, including well-intentioned Christians, would never see the halls of heaven. My older sister was willing to concede that Wesleyan Methodists, Nazarenes and Pilgrim Holiness people might make it, but that was about the sum of it.

Such a position is scarcely a gospel, "good news." But we do indeed have a gospel. Jesus dared to sum up the way to life as an unqualified love for God and neighbor. He said we are to be perfect as God is perfect. How those two injunctions are to be worked out in terms of the instantaneous as well as the never-ending, seems to mandate never-ending exploration. In any case, I cannot imagine that Jesus' epigrammatic encouragements require for their implementation hundreds of U.S. denominations and some 38,000 denominations worldwide (David Barrett's current estimate). If such numbers reflect essential dividedness in the body of Christ, his body is not so much divided as it is atomized.

## The Ironic Partisan

Finally we consider the third stance, that of the ironic partisan. This viewpoint, I repeat, combines *commitment* with *critique oriented toward action.*

Bible-believers know there is no soul without a body. What are the observable truths about us Free Methodists functioning in local churches — each a cell, if you like, in Christ's body? What are those truths which point the way, even if a demanding one, to better health, vigorous vitality, and the fruiting of the Spirit?

I offer four, though with considerable hesitation and tentativity. I do not pretend to global vision or a perfected spirituality. Here is how the ironic partisan sees things:

1. In the last half century we have become materially rich as a church and have not adjusted to this change. As Americans we are intoxicated with our affluence. Our national per capita disposable income, adjusted for inflation, was in 2003 three and a half times what it was in 1947.

As Free Methodists we can rejoice that some good things have happened on the front of ministering to the poor, but for the most part we are unsure how to proceed. Speaking globally, we are preponderantly a church of poverty and of color. We would be wise to speak of a ministry to the rich. Such a ministry to the rich, that is, ourselves, would be the spiritual largesse of the rest of the global Free Methodist family directed our way.

> Globally, we are largely a church of poverty and of color. We would be wise to speak of a ministry to the rich — that is, to us North American Christians.

One sign of vitality in the U.S. church in the past thirty years has been the flourishing of new ethnic churches — Hispanic of several kinds, Haitian, Egyptian, Portuguese. Books are being written on the shift of the center of global Christianity to the developing world. We are positioned exceptionally well to benefit from the ministry of our global partners to us wealth-addled and lukewarm Americans.

I think of an inspiring conference in Kansas City a year or so ago when I was blessed and strengthened by the inspired ministry of our Puerto Rican superintendent, Mercedes Reynoso. In the 2005 Search for the FM Soul gathering I was taught and enriched by our Brazilian Bishop José Ildo.

I think of the extraordinary work being done in northern Illinois by Alma and Juan Cordova and of the great synergy over twenty-five years between Dwight Gregory and ethnic groups of all sorts along the northeastern seaboard.

Our nostalgia and platitudes about ministry to the poor can be more than vapor as the reality of the global Free Methodist family bears in upon us in the U.S. and Canada. We discover the wondrous vibrancy of our urban ethnic churches, are ministered to in our riches, and learn again what it is to minister to the local poor, many of them in our newest churches.

2. Revivalism appears to be an obsolete method of evangelism for the local church. Methodists of all kinds love methods, and now new methods are in order. The Free Methodist Church was founded in a time of revivals.

I grew up, as did many older Free Methodists, when local churches held revivals, with visiting evangelists. But fifteen years ago, while sitting on the FM evangelism commission, I learned we then had only five itinerant evangelists in the field. The Nazarene Church had two hundred. David Clardie, the best paid of our five, had netted $15,000 the previous year.

The day of traditional revival meetings is past. When our pastor asked about our church's hosting a brief revival series, Helen and I sat down and struggled to come up with a single name of a nonbeliever we would find it natural to invite to such a series — rather than to an Alpha group in our home. Tent meetings, street services, protracted meetings in local churches — Do we actually believe we will see conversions that way? And if not, what else is in order?

> Do we still think traditional revival services are the key to conversions? If not, what else is in order?

My wife, who I believe has the gift of evangelism, observes that the typical Free Methodist local church is sadly uninformed about new strategies. But there are many now: The Alpha course (readily adapted if found to be too charismatic); Willow Creek materials and personnel; simple ongoing training from the pulpit in giving personal invitations and sharing one's faith; and, of course, church planting — probably the best of all, though not usually an option for the smaller local church.

Are we really clueless about why many of our local churches do not see a single adult conversion in a year's time? Why do we call ourselves Evangelicals?

3. With the passing of revivalism, our traditional ambivalence about the sacramental as an access to the supernatural

has meant we find ourselves in a number of awkward situations. We tend to be careless in relating the sacrament of the Lord's Supper to spiritual readiness and to the sacrament of baptism. Families go to the front to receive the elements, bringing children who have had no instruction or heart-preparation. We are quite casual about the two sacraments we honor, Holy Communion and baptism.

Without a definite conversion to cite, the early adolescent may come to the traditional time of confirmation wondering what his or her rite of passage is to be. A family in our church, headed by a Jewish Christian, has three sons. Their sons wondered why the church did not have anything like their cousins' Bar Mitzvah.

I mention all this to say that we have halted between two distinct modes of staging the Christian life. One is ordered by the two sacraments — or the Roman and High Anglican tradition of seven, including confirmation, marriage and last rites. The other mode is defined by works of grace and by personal decision. We would be wise to determine how rigorously we follow the instructions of our communion service, how seriously we commend baptism, and how we relate sacraments to personal decision.

We have traditionally not fully trusted the sacramental. In old language, "formalism" typically was a code word for reliance upon sacramental rites rather than the spontaneous outpourings of the Spirit. Such formalism was to be avoided. We seem now to hesitate undecided between a *laissez faire* supernaturalism and a reasonable use of the sacraments as God-ordained instruments of grace. It was by the merest happenstance that I was ever baptized, and that by my grandfather, by sprinkling when I was sixteen. I have no confirming certificate. At our little Cleveland, Ohio, Mt. Pleasant church we saw the district elder four times a year, at which times we enjoyed the Lord's Supper. In contrast, I have Catholic friends who see such benefit in the Mass that they take it daily.

Is the Lord's table something to be visited frequently, after solemn preparation? And what about baptism? How many of our churches, like my own, are obliged to use a nearby borrow pit, or use a neighboring church's portable baptismal tank?

In a word, do we Free Methodists truly believe that the sacraments are efficacious? If so, what is implied for how we make use of them in terms of expectation, preparation, and frequency?

4. I see a disconnect between our teaching about the deeper life in Christ and the conspicuous fact, so evident in church history, that sanctification demands spiritual disciplines and the structures which support such disciplines. We are an undisciplined church, part of a larger American constituency which is also largely undisciplined but is becoming newly aware of the heritage of the disciplines of the Christian life.

Dostoyevsky's young hero, Alyosha (one of the Brothers Karamazov) learns much from an early brief period in the local monastery. He reports that the spiritual life seemed so possible behind the monastery walls, but on his return to town, he was immersed again in the muddle of the commonplace.

We should not ignore history. The deeper life is sustained and cultivated by disciplines. In the past those disciplines often assumed sequestration of some kind, much time together with persons of like commitment, and then a venturing out in unselfish ministry. The more selfless and interventionist the ministry, the greater the need for the disciplines.

The truly challenging disciplines are those of doing, rather than not doing, of action rather than relinquishment. Spiritual exercise such as meditation, along with creative venturing and loving engagement need to be paired with the disciplines of rejection, refusal, abstinence and condemnation. Self-chosen disciplines are the point, rather than rules imposed by others.

We know that the Wesleys got the nickname that stuck, "Methodists," because they were so earnest in their disciplines. No doubt "Methodists" sounds a lot better than "disciplinists," but disciplines are of the essence. The story of B.T. and Ellen Roberts and early Free Methodism makes clear how our soul still is implicated in the models of those early earnest, joyous, enthusiastic, hope-filled, disciplined believers.

I love my church family. I see it is as part of a larger family, in a still larger family. Our soul is, of course, not to be defined apart from God the Holy Spirit. That Spirit is the source of holy purpose and unquenchable hope.

Our mission today as Free Methodists is to tell the truth to one another and to *be* the truth, the Good News of Jesus Christ, in our world. We want the *naive observers* among us to see obvious signs of life. We *partisans* continue to love and deepen our loyalty to the people called Free Methodists while thanking God for the larger global body of Christ. And we *ironic partisans* seek to focus our analysis and concern precisely on helping our church be a humble but effective part of God's redeeming, restoring work in the world.

## CHAPTER 9
# *Reflections and Reactions*

Comments from Symposium Participants

The three Search for the Free Methodist Soul events were conversations, not conferences. Prepared papers were given, but the heart of the gatherings was talking together about what concerns us most as we seek to live as Christians within the family called Free Methodist. Lively conversation filled discussion and meal slots as well as breaks and unscheduled times. And some conversation has continued through email and various chance encounters.

Many participants experienced the gatherings as unusual high points, though some felt frustrated by the lack of closure. Several said the symposiums were the most significant Free Methodist events they ever attended.

The "Search" events succeeded as soundings into the essence and genius of Free Methodism. As somewhat *ad hoc* occasional gatherings they had no official status and were not aimed at coming to defined conclusions.

**Feedback from Symposiums**

The following sampling of feedback from the three gatherings gives a sense of the discussions.

The diversity of responses underscored the liveliness of the denomination's soul. Jennifer Starr-Reivett, for instance, said she had finally arrived at what she felt was a good definition of sanctification, even though it might not be what others thought it was. Meanwhile Bruce Cromwell and Doug Newton maintained that Free Methodists must know their theological roots in order to understand the true value of the denomination.

Jeanne Acheson-Munos asked the church to seek "Jesus Justice" through prayer and holy lives. She related the difficulties of trying to bring Jesus' message to the Haitian people, and the fine line missionaries walk.

Describing her work in home missions, Pastor Bonnie

Braun said she did not want to be part of a church that was defined by what it did *not* do, because such a church was bound to separate itself from the very society it must engage redemptively. While Jeanne Acheson-Munos called for prayer, Braun asked the church to respond to its call to mercy with personnel and money: A home mission representative who could help mobilize and direct compassionate participation by Free Methodist churches across the country.

In his response to Milo Kaufmann, Gerald Bates applauded Kaufmann's effort to delineate the tensions that exist in the denomination and delighted in Kaufmann's conclusion that the soul of the church is the Holy Spirit. However he questioned Kaufmann's assertion that Methodist rationalism, part of the church's DNA, was a manifestation of an unpredictable Holy Spirit.

Different as the responses were, each called the church to holy living and to the ideal that moved the founders and early members — prayer and good works.

**A wide range of issues is stirring the Free Methodist soul.**

A number of respondents mentioned issues, topics, or questions they would like to see addressed in such events. These responses signal the range of issues that are stirring the Free Methodist soul and the diversity of specific concerns. For example:

Have reports on Free Methodist churches that are thriving and how they deal with core issues and doctrines of the denomination.

Give attention to demographic changes in the church.

Focus more on global Free Methodism.

Discuss our role in the larger community of American Protestant denominations.

Focus on servant leadership as modeled by Jesus Christ.

Investigate the early roots of the Christian church and the theological threads that speak to us today.

A passion for souls; reaching out to the lost, who are dying.

Preach the hope of Christ's love!

More worship and prayer.

What does it mean to live a holy life?

How can we teach pastors the necessity of preaching, understanding, and experiencing entire sanctification?

How does the suburban, mostly white Free Methodist Church in the U.S. find its soul?

Does the Free Methodist soul include small, rural community ministries?

Is our soul static or dynamic in relation to changing culture?

How can we encourage people in holiness without legalism?

Does the "Republicanization" of Free Methodism help or hinder our mission?

Explain Wesley's "Plain Account of Christian Perfection."

Develop strategies to address issues.

Deal with diversity of music in worship and different worship styles.

Find the soul of Free Methodism in its emphasis on ministry to the power and empowerment for women and freedom in the Spirit.

More emphasis on cross-cultural ministry.

The essential role of community in sustaining our soul.

Dean Cook, at the time pastor of the Wilmore Free Methodist Church in Kentucky, sent these reflections after the 2004 symposium:

> I thought the resource people and discussion group surfaced a number of important issues: (1) Diversity is diminishing connectionalism. (2) Theology is not the basis for much of our worship. (3) The bishops are not addressing the key issues. (4) Sanctification is a vague doctrine to many, including pastors.
>
> These and other issues need more discussion before focusing on the world. I received some calls from others who regretted not being present. Interest is certain to grow if this is published. ... Keep up the good work. You are onto something good.

Also regarding the first symposium, Milo Kaufmann commented:

I am interested in seeing us define our "soul" not in terms of any unique doctrine (which would be a heresy, of course) but rather in terms of a unique, or at least defining constellation of emphases. My own guess is that such a constellation would include (1) an Arminian (though I wish there were some earlier designation which would work) conception of God's generosity and grace, (2) ministry to the poor and disenfranchised, (3) a stress upon the deeper life in Christ (or earnest Christianity) and (4) a high doctrine of Scripture, which sets us apart from the more rationalistic fringes of the major denominations as well as some of the minor ones.

**A Pastor's Reflection**

The Committee on Free Methodist History and Archives, which organized the three symposiums, asked some of its members for help in assessing the first Search for the Free Methodist Soul. Pastor Bruce Cromwell of the Centralia, Illinois, Free Methodist Church commented at some length; here is a summary of his reflections:

One chorus that seemed to be repeated again and again in the symposium discussion resonates with what is said in the Apostles' Creed. In that great confession we say we "believe in the Holy Spirit, the holy catholic church, the communion of saints, the forgiveness of sins, the resurrection of the body, and the life everlasting."

This is one of the most special phrases in the creed, in our system of belief, for it reminds us that the church is God's creation, not our own. God has given and will continue to give us company so that we will know how rightly to worship. What really is the soul of Free Methodism? I think the answer can be found in an even better question: What does it mean to be part of the church?

Have we somehow missed our calling as Free Methodists simply to the extent that we feel a need to discover and define what makes us distinctive? Perhaps such self-definition forces us to make distinctions that might better be left unmade. As

Free Methodists our real challenge today is not in marking our territory or establishing our sectarian dogmas, but rather in learning how to exist and minister in a world that is no longer dominated by Christendom. In a world that is rapidly losing whatever respect for the church it had, we need to realize that what makes us Christians first and foremost — whether we are Free Methodist, Calvinist, Catholic, or whatever — is our worship of God, our worship through word and sacrament.

We ought to be longing for a recovery of our biblical Christian core. Differences are not unimportant, but what keeps us going and gives us hope is the certain realization that God remembers all those who constitute the communion of the saints, regardless of denominational affiliation.

Still, we do have a story to tell. As inheritors of the Methodist tradition we have the somewhat unique privilege of being able to pick and choose parts of other traditions we like without having to bear the burden of the parts we don't. Look at John Wesley. He took the best and the most beautiful approaches to God from every tradition he encountered to aid himself and the members of his societies in drawing closer to the Lord. I think that's great. Such an approach gives us an ecclesial stance that drops all pretensions of superiority.

So instead of focusing on what makes us different, might we along with Methodist scholars such as Albert Outler, Robert Cushman, Thomas Langford, Geoffrey Wainwright, Will Willimon, and Stanley Hauerwas, recognize that our form of "practical divinity" has both Catholic and Protestant themes?

Catholic with a small "c" simply means "universal," and as Free Methodists we follow in the footsteps of one who borrowed universally from all Christian traditions. In fact, we're more universal even than the Anglican Protestants who gave us birth, since Wesley held to the Eastern fathers in a more determined way than did any of the Western churches before him, Protestant or Catholic.

The great contribution B.T. Roberts made to our faith is that he called us to remember "Old School Methodism," to reflect back upon what Wesley sought to do. As Free Methodists, we embrace anything that authentically draws us closer to

God and true communion with him. We have a particular theological perspective, but we do not restrict the means of grace God chooses to employ in our lives. We simply strive to be as authentic in our relationship with God as we can, and to allow the Holy Spirit to release us from the trappings of sin.

Theological perspective is important. If we want to find our soul, we need only look to the edges of society, to the fringe, to the lost. But if we forget our theological foundations, a generic evangelical flavoring filters into our churches to the point that all that marks us as Free Methodist is the name on the letterhead.

> As Free Methodists, we embrace anything that authentically draws us closer to God and true communion with him.

As Free Methodists we stand squarely within a Wesleyan-Arminian framework. We would do well to reclaim our theological roots. As Methodists, we believe without apology in the centrality of Jesus Christ. We express the need to come to faith through his cross, and to have an experience of conversion. Wesley called the subsequent assurance of salvation the "main doctrine" of the Methodists. But we also believe that once saved we have a responsibility to continue in the covenant of grace and faith with God.

We believe, as James writes, that "faith without works is dead." It is possible for us to forfeit the free gift of salvation through our neglect and irresponsibility. Salvation is indeed through grace, through faith alone, but our condemnation is through our works or lack thereof. That's why we Free Methodists also stress holiness of life, a holiness that can change us both now and permanently.

That's why we Free Methodists also believe in the power of the Holy Spirit. We believe that Pentecost is at the heart of the church and that sanctification can be and should be a reality. Hence we believe in proven structures and disciplines that deepen us and form us into the likeness of God. We have a heart to see justice done and to share the good news with everyone, especially the poor, the alien, the widow.

If we wanted one word to hang our hat on as Free Methodists, we could do a lot worse than "holy." We are called to be a holy people; we are part of a holiness tradition. The definition of holiness I'm coming to appreciate most is found in the first three chapters of the book of Exodus, and specifically in Exodus 3:1-5:

> Moses was tending the flock of Jethro his father-in-law, the priest of Midian, and he led the flock to the far side of the wilderness and came to Horeb, the mountain of God. There the angel of the Lord appeared to him in flames of fire from within a bush. Moses saw that though the bush was on fire it did not burn up. So Moses thought, "I will go over and see this strange sight — why the bush does not burn up."
>
> When the Lord saw that he had gone over to look, God called to him from within the bush, "Moses! Moses!" And Moses said, "Here I am."
>
> "Do not come any closer," God said. "Take off your sandals, for the place where you are standing is holy ground."

What's going on there? Pharaoh had decreed that every boy born to the Hebrews was to be thrown into the Nile and drowned, but Moses' mother saved his young life by casting him into the Nile in a papyrus basket plastered with pitch. She pretended she didn't have a child. After Pharaoh's daughter found the baby among the reeds, she pretended the child was hers. Moses' sister, watching from a distance, pretended to be an innocent bystander and went off in search of a nursemaid — Moses' real mother, pretending to be just a nursemaid.

Moses continued this line of pretending, killing an Egyptian who was beating a Hebrew and then pretending that he hadn't, burying the body in the sand.

All this pretense continued until the moment when Moses in the wilderness stepped into the presence of a holy God. Everything suddenly became clear. This is holiness: Standing before God and removing all our pretense. No masks. No games. Being simply who we are, in the presence of the One who simply is.

What is the soul of Free Methodism? I pray that more than anything it's being holy and pure, faithful and true. That's a very important quality.

Now, we do of course have important distinctives to address. Can we discuss issues such as frequency of communion, and infant baptism or infant dedication? We may well disagree. But the church needs to be constantly informed and reformed from within by a community of earnest believers in whose corporate life the Spirit of God is peculiarly at work, just as it was in the earliest Christian communities.

That's how John Wesley saw his societies. They weren't supposed to be rivals of the Church of England but fellowships of earnest Christians within it who by their corporate effort would restore to the church that apostolic witness it seemed to lack. Reformation from within. Working together to bring salvation to the world.

As Will Willimon reminds us, from the very beginning Christianity was not primarily a doctrine but a community. The first Christians not only proclaimed good news; they formed a new community, distinct and particular, a place of growth and formation to which members were called. *Koinonia*, fellowship, was the basic category of Christian existence.

Upon joining a church people ceased to worry about "my" needs and began to find concern for "our" needs. They felt themselves closely knit together in a unity that radically transcended the human boundaries of race, culture, and social rank. They were brothers and sisters to each other, members of one body, the body of Christ.

Body of Christ — that was the phrase Paul used to summarize the common experience of the faithful. As Free Methodists, are we sectarian? Are we exclusive? No. The church has never cared whether anyone is a member of the tribe as long as that membership does not prevent one from sharing the table of the Lord.

But we are committed also to being a community capable of sustaining one another in our struggle against the world. After all, we are part of a Methodist movement that by accident became a church. If we're not about the unity of the church, as Hauerwas has suggested, we're not about anything.

Our unity as Free Methodists is found in our mystical union with Jesus Christ grounded in a life of prayer. Our central concern should be whether or not we are feeding the hungry, clothing the naked, and visiting the sick and imprisoned.

As Free Methodists we must be committed to worshipping the Lord in spirit and in truth. Worship is accepting whatever mysteries and wonders God brings our way. It is leaving self-consciousness and pretension at the door and having a social consciousness where the "I" becomes the "we."

Here we find the richness of Free Methodism, for the Free Methodist understands that more important than being a part of this church is being a part of Jesus' church. We're a part of something much bigger than ourselves. We're connected to brothers and sisters throughout the world and through the ages who have responded to God's Spirit moving in their midst. It just happens that we are right here, right now.

What is the soul of Free Methodism? A Free Methodist is someone who works with others to draw closer to the presence of Christ. A Free Methodist is someone who hopes more than anything to one day hear the Lord say, "Well done." A Free Methodist is someone who understands that when everything is said and done, everything the Free Methodist Church says and does is done because God matters. And hopefully our work will matter, too.

## Another Reflection

Another member of the Committee on Free Methodist History and Archives, Pastor Kathy Callahan Howell from Cincinnati, reflected as follows on the first symposium:

By the end of the time together we were asking whether we should try to be unique or the same as other churches. We wanted to focus on how we are alike — basic Christianity. I see the value of this line of thinking. However I do not want to see us abandon our heritage of uniqueness.

As a young woman I became disenchanted with the "organized church" due to its many divisions. I still believe that the ideal would be one Bride, a fully universal church. However I began to also see how God took our brokenness, the church's inability to remain unified, and used that reality to create various expressions of the body of Christ which were able to meet the needs of different people.

The transforming power of holiness and the priority of the poor: These focus our mission in a positive direction. Though I applaud the affirmation of our common beliefs, I think we do well to retain our distinctives in two main areas:

> The transforming power of holiness and the priority of the poor: These focus our mission in a positive direction.

Sometimes it is more important to ask the right questions than to find particular answers. I felt that the greatest value of the symposium was beginning to define the questions we need to be asking ourselves.

### An Editor's Summation

Finally, a word from Doug Newton, editor of *Light and Life Magazine*. In response to the first symposium, Doug wrote:

I thought this conference was about the most important one I've been involved with in the last couple of years. It contrasts particularly with a couple of high-level meetings, such as a strategic planning task force meeting I participated in. It was really important that a meeting be held that was asking key questions about our identity. In contrast, the strategic task force was immediately jumping to goals without dealing with key issues of identity and mission.

People have been asking the question of who we are for years. That question has been getting answered in informal ways, but having an event to get the ball rolling to think about it more broadly was great.

Probably many people would have liked more closure, even though we hadn't come to a definition. The discussion ended so divergent that people couldn't see what we accomplished. A summary of progress and some convergent statements at the end would have added value to the gathering.

I came away wishing that every one of our conference superintendents had been here.

## CHAPTER 10
# Seven Keys to Free Methodist Renewal

Howard A. Snyder
Professor of Wesley Studies
Tyndale Seminary, Toronto

The Search for the Free Methodist Soul events, by design, did not come to any definite conclusions. And yet significant insights emerged.

In light of the three "Search" gatherings, this chapter provides an interpretation of Free Methodist history and identity, then suggests seven practical steps that could lead to renewed vigor in our tradition.

**Interpreting Free Methodist History**

In the Bible, "soul" does not mean "spirit" (contrasted with "body" or "flesh") but rather *person*. A person's *soul* is their true identity, what makes me "me" and you "you." It means all that makes us human — body, mind, and spirit. The human person is not an "individual" (someone "divided" from others and "indivisible"). That's the modern myth. Rather humans are social beings who find their true identity in interaction with others (think of children with their parents and siblings) and in interaction with God.

So also with the "Free Methodist soul." We don't mean some strange, otherworldly spiritual quality. We mean those marks that make us truly Free Methodist, that make up the particular *charism* (grace-calling or vocation) of Free Methodism-in-mission. This is a social reality. Free Methodism is not basically an organization or institution or even a tradition. It is *people* — people-in-mission in fulfillment of our special calling — or else people-out-of-mission, needing to be called back and ahead to mission.

The "search for the Free Methodist soul," then, is an inquiry into the nature of our *calling together* and our *calling forward* for the sake of God's work of redemption and new creation.

**Reaffirming Mission.** If one point of consensus emerged in the whole Search process, it was the reaffirmation of Free Methodism's historic sense of mission. B.T. Roberts and early Free Methodist *Disciplines* put it this way: Our "mission is twofold — to maintain the Bible standard of Christianity, and to preach the Gospel to the poor." I've heard that kind of language more in the last ten years than in the previous fifty. Something is stirring.

Many people are saying the same thing in different ways. Pastor Kathy Callahan Howell put it this way: "We do well to retain our distinctives in two main areas, the transforming power of holiness and the priority of the poor" in order to focus "mission in a positive direction."

B.T. Roberts' formulation was profound in its simplicity: "Maintain the Bible standard of Christianity and preach the Gospel to the poor." By the "Bible standard" Roberts meant holiness, surely, but he meant it in a particular sense. For Roberts, Bible Christianity meant being like Jesus (living the mind of Christ) and doing what Jesus did — personally and as a people. Holiness is Christlikeness — nothing more, nothing less. That means *action* and *mission*. So Roberts throughout life kept pointing to what Jesus did in fulfilling his own mission. He kept pointing to the Jesus who said, "The Spirit of the Lord is upon me, because he has anointed me to bring good news to the poor" (Luke 4:18, NRSV).

In Roberts' mind, biblical Christianity and the gospel for the poor overlapped. They merge into one when we truly focus on Jesus Christ and live by his Spirit.

This way of putting mission is not explicitly Wesleyan, but it is certainly Wesleyan in spirit. And perhaps this is the point: Not to need to be specific or particular about being Wesleyan, but to be Wesleyan by doing what Wesley and B.T. Roberts sought to do: Be faithful to Jesus Christ and Scripture. Seek first, in actual practice, the kingdom of God and its justice *now* in the present world, understanding that that's where heaven and eternal life begin; where they overlap. Bear witness to Jesus' good news with and among the poor and oppressed. Be a *people* and a movement that does this.

**Four Stages.** Like Methodism and other Christian traditions, Free Methodism started out as a movement. Looking back (and simplifying somewhat), we can identify four stages in Free Methodist history. These phases are quite clearly marked in the church's ethos, self-understanding, institutions, leading personalities, and even statistics, and can be illustrated as follows:

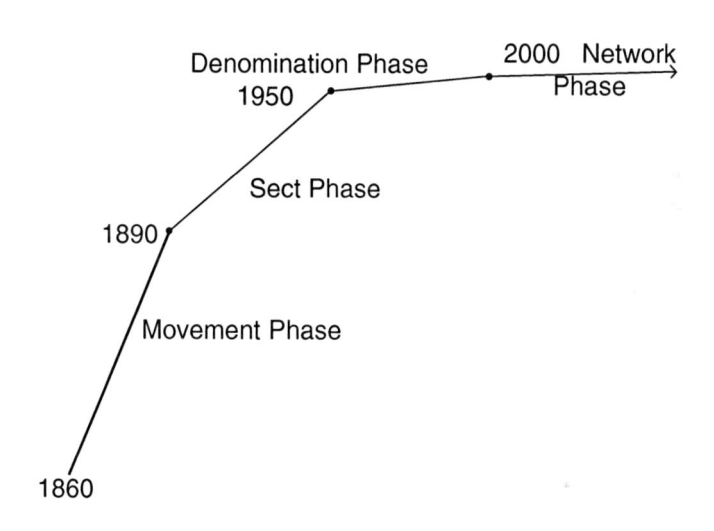

```
                Denomination Phase      2000  Network
                     1950                     Phase

                     Sect Phase
         1890

              Movement Phase

   1860
```

I. *Movement Phase (1860-1890)*. The Free Methodist Church grew rapidly from 1860 to about 1890. Membership growth, the multiplication of congregations and conferences, abundant reports of revival, and other evidence show that for its first thirty years, Free Methodism was indeed movemental. The most rapid growth came in the sixteen years from 1874 to 1890, when total membership went from 7,603 to 21,161 — about 178 percent growth over the three quadrennia. If growth had continued at near this rate, the denomination would have had some 2,000,000 members in North America by the time of its centennial in 1960, whereas total North American membership that year was about 60,000 and worldwide membership was about 100,000.

II. *Sect Phase (1890-1950)*. With the death of B.T. Roberts (1893), the rejection of women's ordination in 1890, and the loss of the Pentecost Bands, the denomination turned increasingly inward. Whereas John Wesley stressed "all inward *and outward* holiness," Free Methodists in this period focused more inward than outward, narrowing the outward to a few specifics of dress, entertainment, and personal habits. The negative side of this is often lamented, but Free Methodist sectarianism also served a positive function. It enhanced group identity and solidarity. You knew what it meant to be Free Methodist. The "legalisms" served a positive function much as did Salvation Army uniforms and Roman Catholic monastic habits.

Foreign missions flourished during this phase, but in North America Free Methodist inwardness constricted mission and limited growth.

III. *Denomination Phase (1950-2000).* The principal markers of the denomination phase were two: (1) a shift from agreed, shared disciplines (particularly regarding dress, entertainment, church attendance and devotional life) to individualistic and largely undefined "personal convictions," and relatedly, (2) a drift toward generic, politically conservative U.S. evangelicalism. *Few Free Methodists living today can understand or remember this transition.*

Although other factors were at work, the main impulses behind this shift were the cultural impact of World War II, the subsequent rise of an affluent and largely suburban middle-class society, and popular entertainment technology. The Free Methodist kid who grew up on a farm in Michigan or in a lower-class neighborhood in Chicago went off to the war, saw the world, came home and married, got a college education on the GI Bill, and became a public school teacher in a growing suburb. The whole denomination shifted, losing its countercultural ethos. Free Methodists abandoned most of their denominational markers (lipstick? plain dress? prayer meeting?) and mostly became generic evangelicals. Because of the popularity of very conservative Calvinist dispensational thinking, typified by Hal Lindsey's *Late Great Planet Earth,* Frank Peretti's *This Present Darkness,* and the *Left Behind* novels, many Free Methodists unknowingly became non-Wesleyan dispensationalists. We absorbed an unbiblical "rapture" theology that was suspicious of efforts at social reform, hostile to environmental concerns, and mostly negative toward women's leadership.

As a denomination, Free Methodism cast about for definitions of success to replace its historic sense of mission. Options partially embraced from time to time included Church Growth, charismatic leadership and styles, business models such as Management By Objective, megachurch models, Vineyard approaches, Seeker Sensitivity, and the Purpose-Driven Church.

But recently we have seen more encouraging signs: New emphasis on our historic mission, especially among the poor, ethnic church planting in the U.S., new growth in Free Methodist world missions, and the prospering of some of our "overseas" Free Methodist general conferences and of our educational institutions in the United States.

Perhaps the most prophetic recent development is the increasing numbers of women in leadership. If B.T. Roberts was right, this is a long-range road to renewal. The "comparative failure of Christianity" to transform the world, Roberts said, is because women "are not permitted to labor according to their ability, for the spread of the Gospel." If women had "been given, since the days of the first Apostles, the same rights as men, this would be quite another world" (*Ordaining Women* [1891; 2003 reprint], 79-82).

Was Roberts right? We may yet find out, at least so far as Free Methodism is concerned. The Free Methodist Church is one of a very few conservative denominations that ordain women. In the context of American evangelicalism, we are still countercultural at least on that point.

IV. *Network Phase (2000-??).* American Protestantism has entered what some call a "post-denominational" phase. The roots of this lie in the anti-institutionalism of the late Sixties and early Seventies, but also in the increased individualism, "localism," and material prosperity of past decades. Ironically (but typically), as evangelical Christians have become more prosperous they have given away proportionately less of their income, and more of their church giving has remained local rather than denominational or global.

These larger currents have touched us also. Major Free Methodist denominational structures have been dismantled; annual conferences have been reorganized, renamed, or merged; denominational identity and loyalty have withered. As Dean Cook put it, "Diversity is diminishing connectionalism." Free Methodism in the United States has become a loose network of local churches pursuing their own agendas and also involved in various other networks. Overall the church has gotten more congregational than episcopal or connectional. Free Methodism today is a network and a network of networks rather than a movement, sect, or denomination.

This shift is both a concern and an opening. Networks can be dynamic, given effective leadership and the renewing work of the Spirit. Networks usually are more flexible than are hierarchical or institutional structures, so they are open to change — for good or ill.

These four phases and shifts sprang from a combination of internal and external factors, as I've hinted. They were partly a response to developments in the larger culture, but they also reflect "normal" cycles often observed in religious, social, and even political movements. Yet this is not predestination; these shifts result from choices people make as they negotiate the narrow path between being *in* the world or *of* it.

### The Free Methodist Synthesis

Methodists like to talk about the so-called "Wesleyan Quadrilateral" of Scripture, reason, tradition, and experience. I propose a different kind of quadrilateral (or square) to illustrate the strengths and dilemmas of Free Methodist identity (as illustrated on page 145).

The strange thing about Wesleyans, and particularly Free Methodists, is that they don't fit neatly into the main categories of Christian history. In a sense they are a hybrid of four traditions: Anglican, evangelical, charismatic, and Anabaptist. Free Methodists are *evangelicals*, but only in some ways. They are *charismatic* in one sense but not in another. They have *Anabaptist* (radical Protestant) roots through Moravianism but also *Roman Catholic* roots through Anglicanism. A complex DNA.

These four diverse traditions, each contributing to the Free Methodist synthesis, have contrasting ways of understanding worship, sacrament, evangelism, community, discipleship, and mission. Each tradition views the church's role in culture differently. The dynamics can vary also in different cultural contexts. For example, liturgical sacramental worship was once "culture" (in England and in medieval Europe), but in many American Protestant churches has become "counterculture." (Interestingly, a focus on the gospel for the poor has almost always been countercultural, and affirming women in leadership generally has been, as well.)

When Free Methodists ask about their soul or identity, they thus draw on one or more of these four traditions. So the Free Methodist soul can be mapped as follows:

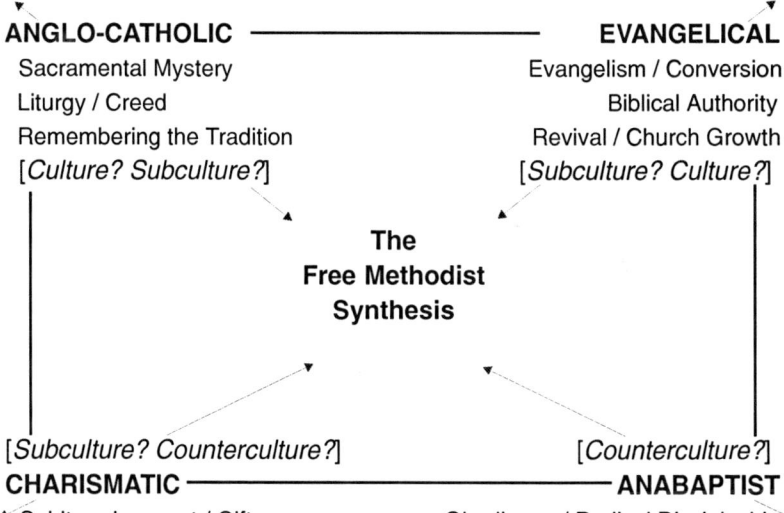

**ANGLO-CATHOLIC** ——————— **EVANGELICAL**
Sacramental Mystery — Evangelism / Conversion
Liturgy / Creed — Biblical Authority
Remembering the Tradition — Revival / Church Growth
*[Culture? Subculture?]* — *[Subculture? Culture?]*

**The Free Methodist Synthesis**

*[Subculture? Counterculture?]* — *[Counterculture?]*
**CHARISMATIC** ——————— **ANABAPTIST**
Spirit-endowment / Gifts — Obedience / Radical Discipleship
Emotion / Ecstasy / "Getting Blessed" — Ethical Responsibility
Sanctification / Living in Love — Social Justice / Gospel to Poor

In this picture, the converging arrows point to the authentic Free Methodist soul, the hard-to-maintain Free Methodist synthesis. The diverging corner arrows show what happens when one of the four traditions "wins" over the others. The FM person or congregation moves away from its historic soul to an exaggerated emphasis. The disaffected Free Methodist (person or congregation) becomes Anglican, Calvinist conservative, charismatic, or joins the Mennonites or some radical discipleship community.

Where do you or I — or our parents or our grandparents, our children, or church — fit on this map? A little reflection reveals the range of possibilities. Free Methodist history shows, I think, that the closer we get to the center, the more fully we embody the authentic Free Methodist soul.

Yet that soul is big enough to embrace a broad range. Some committed Free Methodists feel at home toward the upper left of the map. They deeply appreciate tradition, sacrament, and liturgy. Others find themselves at the lower right, embracing radical discipleship, social justice, and ministry to and among the poor, with less emphasis on creed and sacrament.

Charismatic Free Methodists celebrate our historic emphasis on living by and in the Spirit. Free Methodists who see themselves primarily as evangelicals stress conversion and biblical authority over discipleship, sacrament, or counter-cultural witness.

Is it not clear, though, that Free Methodism at its best combines all these? Has this not always been true of the Free Methodist Church at its best?

Certainly this was true of John Wesley. In fact, this is the heart of the remarkable Wesleyan synthesis; part of the genius of Wesley's optimism of grace. Though with somewhat different accents, this synthesis was the genius also of B.T. and Ellen Roberts.

> **Renewal means helping our people experience the Free Methodist *synthesis* and *practice* the Free Methodist calling.**

If this map is accurate, then renewing the Free Methodist soul means helping our congregations understand and *experience* authentic Free Methodism. It means helping our people experience the Free Methodist synthesis and practice the Free Methodist charism, maintaining the Bible standard of Christianity and preaching the gospel to the poor.

**Our Default Identity**

Free Methodism identity can be pictured in another way: What is the "glue" that holds us together? Where do we really find our center, our sense of identity?

We trust, of course, that we find our center in Jesus Christ, made real to us by the Holy Spirit. But how do we picture Jesus Christ and the work of the Spirit? Our understanding of Jesus Christ doesn't come to us directly from the Bible; like everyone else, we get it partly through our heritage, our family tradition. And that tradition, that story, is shaped by past and present stories and contexts.

Jesus, the church, and the gospel itself are shaped for us by the interplay of four parts of the Christian life: *Doctrine, piety, liturgy,* and *ethics*. Our sense and source of identity is found in some combination of these four dimensions. So the Christian life generally, and a church's sense of identity, can be pictured in this way:

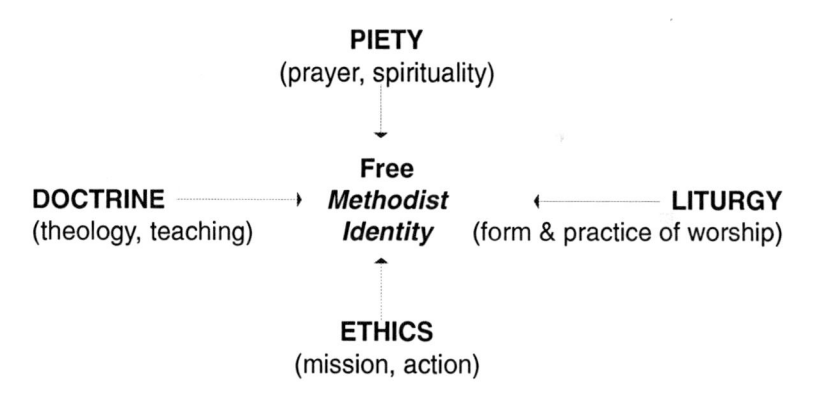

**PIETY**
(prayer, spirituality)

**DOCTRINE** ⟶ *Free Methodist Identity* ⟵ **LITURGY**
(theology, teaching)  (form & practice of worship)

**ETHICS**
(mission, action)

These four are all connected, of course, because all involve both thought and action. They overlap. Piety includes the ethical dimension, doctrine informs liturgy, and ethics shapes how we worship.

In most churches and denominations, however, one of these four tends to be strongest. One of the four, generally, is the default position to which, when push comes to shove, the church moves. This element provides the primary sociological bond; the strongest glue. Some churches put the greatest emphasis on doctrine; others on ethics, or liturgy, or piety.

So a *pietistic church* places the biggest accent on spiritual experience. A *doctrinal church* centers its life and existence in its creed or statement of faith. A *liturgical church* finds its identity in its worship practices, often (but not always) centering in the sacraments. An *ethics-centered church* stresses the way Christians should actually live in the world and usually focuses especially on Jesus as our example.

What holds Free Methodism together? What is the glue? Where do we find our center?

This will vary, no doubt, from church to church and from region to region. My observation however is that most Free Methodists find their identity in piety more than in the other three. Doctrine, worship, and ethical action are all important, but spiritual or devotional experience trumps the others.

Consider this thought experiment. In a Free Methodist gathering, four Christians who are essentially unknown to the congregation each give their testimony. The first emphasizes the importance of sound doctrine. The second speaks of the centrality of worship. The third talks of being witnesses in society. The fourth talks of his or her daily time of prayer and Bible reading.

Which person (without the congregation knowing more) will be seen as the most authentic, the best Christian? In most Free Methodist churches, I think, it would be the pietist — the one who most quickly and persuasively testifies to deep personal spiritual experience. We are more impressed by spiritual experience than by doctrine, ethics, or liturgy.

Or consider this: In a typical Free Methodist sermon (if there is such), where will the preacher end up? What kind of application or appeal will be made? In my experience, at least, nine times out of ten the appeal will be to piety. That is, it will be an appeal to more prayer, or deeper dedication or rededication — essentially to some private and individual spiritual transaction with God. It is less likely to be a appeal to doctrine ("Believe this; be convinced of this"), or liturgy ("Begin worshiping in this way"), or ethics ("Change your behavior; live out your faith in this way"). I have heard all four kinds of appeals, but the pietist one is the run-away favorite.

This is natural enough. Methodism from the first has been a pietist movement, influenced by Continental Pietism. But Methodism, and certainly John Wesley, were always strongly action oriented, as well. Piety and devotion were never ends in themselves; they were the *means* toward loving God with all our heart, soul, strength, and mind, and our neighbors as ourselves. They were means of grace. Wesley's insistent emphasis on "all inward and outward holiness" was a way of holding piety and mission together; a missional piety. That's partly why Wesley and his followers were called Methodists, not Pietists.

As Free Methodists we tend to collapse mission into piety. Devotion becomes the meaning of mission, and the goal of mission is to make us more pious. During Free Methodism's thirty-year "movement phase" piety and mission were arguably more in balance than today, despite some excesses.

> Can we learn to practice a more missional piety — "all inward *and outward* holiness" — rather than allowing inward spirituality to substitute for outward mission?

Perhaps the malady that affected Free Methodism during its sect phase was not so much legalism as a too inwardly-focused pietism.

It is not either/or. Piety is essential. But our piety should be informed and shaped by doctrine, liturgy, and missional ethics. Vital Free Methodism that incarnates comprehensive mission will be all these things: Pietistic, biblically doctrinal, healthily liturgical, and missionally ethical. Can we learn to practice a more missional piety — "all inward *and outward* holiness" — rather than allowing inward spirituality to substitute for outward mission?

Yes, we can. This discussion is really all prelude to several suggestions for renewed Free Methodism vitality today.

## Seven Steps toward Free Methodist Renewal

The following suggestions are based in three realities: The nature of gospel and church as revealed in Scripture, Wesleyan theology, and our own history and heritage. Note that these seven proposals for renewed life and mission for the Free Methodist Church are not quick fixes, because renewal and spirituality do not come by quick fixes.

**1. Build Free Methodist community and identity in our seminaries and colleges.**

I became much more a Free Methodist while a student at interdenominational Asbury Seminary in the 1960s. The reason was the Free Methodist community there, centered in the local church and the John Wesley Seminary Foundation. The sixty or so FM students at Asbury got acquainted, formed friendships with Free Methodist professors, and developed networks that have continued until today.

But things have changed. Now I find very little Free Methodist community and denominational socialization and visioning at Asbury, except as occurs incidentally in the local church.

A primary reason is that our denomination now affiliates with several seminaries, not just Asbury, and has almost totally dismantled the John Wesley Seminary Foundation as an identity-mission-vision-building community. At least at Asbury, FM students often emerge from seminary *less*, rather than *more*, Free Methodist.

This could change. All it would take is intentional and adequately funded leadership at every seminary where ten or more Free Methodist students are found. With denominational leadership from bishops, conference superintendents, and the denominational structure generally, men and women could be emerging from our seminaries year by year with vision and enthusiasm for Free Methodist mission and a taste of Free Methodist community, excited to live the Free Methodist synthesis and embody its charism.

Currently this is being done more effectively in some of our colleges than in seminaries. But more attention to FM mission, vision, and community needs to happen across the educational spectrum. This would bear rich fruit over generations. It would not change things overnight. But wise steps and prudent investment in this direction now could mean a renewed church in 2050.

**2. Develop leaders through mentoring.**

Christian leadership is about character and discipleship, not primarily about knowledge and skills. That's why Jesus trained the Apostles by being with them for three years, discipling and mentoring them. The Free Methodist Church must do the same.

Seminary can't do it alone, even with programs of "supervised" or "mentored" ministry. The only way to develop leaders who understand and are excited about the Free Methodist synthesis and charism is to mentor them through a relatively seamless process.

Some ways to do this:

- Assign experienced, theologically well-grounded pastors to mentor (personally, relationally) every ministerial candidate through to the time of ordination. The process should include whatever years the person may spend in college or seminary.
- Implement a three-year mentoring process for all new pastors. Every new pastor should be discipled (personally, relationally) by an experienced pastor (active or retired) who has proven to be effective and spiritually mature and who owns the Free Methodist heritage.
- Assign pastoral mentors to pastors who are leading struggling or at-risk congregations.
- In the mentoring process, focus in four main areas: (1) building community, (2) equipping Christians for ministry in the world, (3) spiritual growth and integration, and (4) deeper grounding in our own tradition. The means should be learning by doing, not primarily learning by reading or by intellectually learning concepts.

The assumption here is that the primary task of pastors is to build up the body of Christ and to equip the body (and all its members) to be God's mission in the world. This kind of discipling-mentoring is required if the biblical vision of the church (particularly in Ephesians 4:1-16 and 1 Corinthians 12-14) is ever to become operational.

3. **Focus the conference superintendent's role on pastoral mentoring, renewing existing churches, and church planting.**

Conference superintendents are above all else pastors to pastors. Their role is well summarized by the Apostle Paul in his admonition to the Ephesian elders: "Keep watch over yourselves and all the flock of which the Holy Spirit has made you overseers. Be shepherds of the church of God, which he bought with his own blood" (Acts 20:28; the whole passage, verses 17-35, is important for mentoring).

This approach will gradually become easier, of course, asced the first two suggestions outlined earlier begin to bear fruit. Only discipled pastors, in most cases, can become mentoring superintendents.

The measure of success of a conference superintendent should be the number of pastors effectively encouraged and mentored, the number of existing congregations revitalized for mission, and the number of new churches effectively planted, especially among the poor. The process will not work if middle-class megachurches are the model. We now have plenty of evidence that real movements multiply small but lively congregations, not superchurches.

Early Free Methodists understood well that they were not called to build "popular" churches (today called megachurches). If megachurches happen by accident as a result of faithful ministry, that is both a cause for celebration and a red flag — because (another sociological principle) growing numbers mean declining personal commitment unless the church is honeycombed with discipleship-and-ministry cells.

In other words, the role of superintendents is a larger version of the role of pastors. They are to help equip pastors and congregations for the work of ministry (Eph. 4:11-12).

This has implications also for bishops. Above all, bishops are pastors of the larger flock. Their primary role is not administrative but pastoral and inspirational. They are to pastor (mentor, instruct, encourage) superintendents so they can pastor the pastors who pastor (guide and equip for ministry) the local congregations. Administration is of course necessary but must be secondary and functional for mission.

4. **Reinvent the early Methodist class meeting.**

The class and band meetings of early Methodism were key to its vitality, growth, and staying power. Yet (as I explain in *Populist Saints*), Free Methodism never really experienced the class meeting the way it functioned in early Methodism. By B.T. Roberts' day the class meeting had lost its original function.

All vital churches (at least in North America) have some form of effective small-group, cell-group, or home-group structure. Denomination-wide, the Free Methodist Church has never had such a structure, even though for generations the *Discipline* made provision for such and required class-meeting participation.

We need a contemporary functional equivalent of the class meeting. A class meeting is not a Sunday School class, a Bible study group, or a group for fellowship and prayer only. It is a structure of accountability with agreed-upon rules (that is, a covenant including specific disciplines).

The class meeting needs to be reinvented for our day and made part of basic Free Methodist structure. It should include specific disciplines that cover key areas such as time use, financial stewardship, family relationships, witness, and creation care. Only in such contexts of face-to-face community can questions like these be effectively (relationally, not legalistically) faced:

Am I honoring God in my financial stewardship?
What guidelines do I and my children follow with regard to television, the Internet, movies, and other forms of entertainment?
Am I spending time daily in prayer and Bible study?
Am I caring for God's creation in practical ways, such as recycling?
How am I involved with God's mission globally and locally?
How am I contributing to the life and mission of our local church?
How are my relationships with family and coworkers?
Am I growing in my love toward God and others?

How am I living out the Free Methodist synthesis and calling?
Am I using my gifts for mission and to God's glory?
How is my life benefiting the poor and oppressed of the world?
Is the work I do in my job or employment consistent with the values of the kingdom of God?

If we do not answer these questions in the context of loving, accountable community, we probably don't *really* answer them at all.

A special denominational task force could design a Free Methodist form of class meeting for today. Participation in such groups should be mandatory, not optional, for all adult members. If this were implemented, the result is predictable: More highly committed and countercultural Free Methodists; slow membership growth initially but steadily increasing growth over time.

Reinventing the class meeting ties in nicely with the discipling/mentoring emphasis above. We will get more mature, more committed, and more effective pastors, for example, once the denomination begins to reap the fruit of families formed in this kind of environment. Mentoring — informal and effective — begins here, in local churches and in small groups.

**5. Tell our story; rehearse the history.**

Earlier chapters in this book, particularly those by Doug Newton and Stan Ingersol, show how important it is to tell and retell our family history — as part of the larger story of rescue and redemption that God is accomplishing.

We live today in a world of competing, compelling, life-shaping (and life-warping) stories. The most potent narratives come to us through television, the Internet, and advertising. Today these are mostly merging into one. Increasingly entertainment, news reporting, and Internet communication are all forms of marketing. "Everything for sale," as one book title puts it. Do we want our children and our churches to be shaped morally by manipulative market myths, or by the counter-story of the gospel of the kingdom and the way it has come to us through the Free Methodist synthesis and charism?

Telling our story means sharing personal testimonies of God at work in our lives. Early Methodism thrived in part on the testimonies, the stories, of God's transforming grace in people's experiences. There is something refreshing and renewing in hearing Christians share how God has worked and is working in their own stories. The trick, then, is to tie these testimonies to the larger story of our church through history. The old testimony meeting can be reinvented as we see how each person's particular story fits into the larger narrative of God at work.

We need to tell each other our story in bite-sized chunks, in anecdotes and incidents, as every vital culture does. We need to see how the little stories fit into the larger story. This includes, importantly, what God has done and is doing through Free Methodists around the world.

Resources are already available; what is needed now is the *doing* and *telling*. That is one key function of the other steps mentioned earlier — building community, mentoring, discipling one another relationally. Stories shape behavior when we rehearse them *in community*, in the family. They don't much change behavior if they remain merely printed or archived.

So the Free Methodist story — part of the larger Christian story of creation, redemption, and new creation — should filter its way into our shared life. It should be woven into sermons, retold in families and small groups, shared in membership classes, and required in pastoral training. In bite-sized chunks.

As part of the larger story, our story will keep repeating the originating vision of Free Methodism: "to maintain the Bible standard of Christianity, and to preach the gospel to the poor." This does not so much need to be reinterpreted as to be repeated and practiced.

**6. Teach holiness as the mind of Christ through the fullness of the Spirit.**

Holiness as Christlikeness must still be our emphasis. But there is no good reason to continue using the language of "perfection" or "entire sanctification." This is so for three reasons: (1) the terms are not the only or even the primary ones used in

Scripture for holiness; (2) the terms were problematic even in Wesley's day; and (3) today the terms do not communicate what the Bible actually teaches.

Even proponents of entire sanctification today often misunderstand what Wesley meant. The term "perfection" doesn't mean for us what it meant for Wesley or the biblical writers. We think of *perfection* as something that cannot be improved upon, something without flaw. What Wesley meant however was *perfecting* — constant living and growing in grace. We don't use "perfect" that way today. Wesley meant perfection in the dynamic biblical sense, not the static contemporary sense.

Since the Bible offers a range of terms, let's use those that best communicate today. Wesley said Christian perfection meant having the mind of Christ; being conformed to Jesus' image; walking as he walked. These are biblical terms. "Mind of Christ" means much more than "a Christ-like attitude." It means Christ-like mission; experiencing the missional mind that Jesus showed, focused on one goal: That God might be glorified through the coming of his kingdom on earth, as in heaven. (Note how Jesus speaks of his own mission in the Gospel of John.)

For Wesley, entire sanctification was practical Christlikeness enabled by the Holy Spirit, generally involving a second spiritual step or crisis beyond conversion. The phrase that perhaps best captures this today is: Living the mind of Christ through the fullness of the Spirit. "Mind of Christ" (1 Cor. 2:16 and related passages), "mind of the Spirit" (Rom. 8:27) and "fullness" (John 1:16; Eph. 1:23, 3:19, 4:13; Col. 1:19 and other passages) are key biblical terms. Paul says Christians "have been given fullness in Christ" (Col. 2:10) and exhorts believers to "be filled with the Spirit" (Eph. 5:18).

The beauty of the New Testament term "fullness" is that it unites three related dimensions: Personal infilling with the Spirit, the fullness of Jesus Christ in the church, and the fullness of Jesus Christ in all creation. It is the whole church together that grows up into Christ, "attaining to the whole measure of the fullness of Christ" (Eph. 4:13). No Christian attains to the fullness of Christ alone, but as we are filled with the

Spirit, we grow up into Jesus, truly becoming his Spirit-filled body. Usually this involves both crisis and process and is facilitated by small-group community.

This is hugely practical. We can help believers come to know Jesus Christ deeply through the infilling of the Spirit and through life together in Christian community — and thus through redemptive mission in the world in fulfillment of Jesus' words, "As the Father has sent me, I am sending you" (John 20:21).

This is what John Wesley meant by "all inward and outward holiness" — loving God with heart, strength, soul, and mind, and our neighbors (near and far) as ourselves.

The meaning of entire sanctification can be reborn. The Bible shows the way and provides the language. In church history, a renewed experience of the Holy Spirit has often come through finding new but biblically authentic language that communicates well in the cultural context.

**7. Emphasize the mission and kingdom of God, focusing on the gospel for the poor.**

God calls the Free Methodist Church not to serve itself — not merely to grow, and not to cave in to consumerist culture. God calls us to his mission in the world — the mission of the Trinity: God the Father sending the Son into the world in the power of the Holy Spirit to bring redemption and new creation. He calls and invites us into his mission.

It is not so much that the Free Methodist Church has a mission as that God's mission has a church. Our part of that church is the people called Free Methodist. So "seeking first the kingdom of God and its justice" (Mt. 6:31) means fulfilling our part of God's mission.

The kingdom of God is the big picture. It is God's sure goal (his will done on earth as in heaven) and his master plan: all things in heaven and earth reconciled and healed through Jesus Christ (Eph. 1:10; Col. 1:20). And this is being accomplished in significant measure "through the church" (Eph. 3:10). As we are faithful to God, we know where we are headed: "The earth will be filled with the knowledge of the Lord as the waters cover the sea" (Isa. 11:9). The Messiah "will not falter or be discouraged till he establishes justice on earth" (Isa. 42:2).

The Bible says a key sign of God's kingdom and effective mission is that good news is brought to the poor. This was B.T. Roberts' key insight. It is the charism of Free Methodism and thus key to Free Methodist renewal today.

In 2004 Free Methodist World Missions published a significant 63-page document, *A Theology of Mission for Free Methodist World Missions*, edited by Dan Sheffield. This excellent resource dovetails nicely with the focus on mission I am suggesting here.

## Conclusion

These seven steps can breathe new life into the Free Methodist Church over time. We know this because they are all biblical and practical: Building community in our FM schools, developing leaders through mentoring, refocusing the superintendent's role, reinventing the class meeting, rehearsing our story, teaching holiness as the mind of Christ through the Spirit, and emphasizing mission in terms of the kingdom of God.

This is not the whole picture, of course. Much could be said on other issues: Sacraments, worship and liturgy, "traditional," "contemporary," and "blended" musical styles, economic and ecological justice, ways of evangelism, and particular doctrinal concerns. But given the phases of our history, these seven steps are decisive today.

The search for the Free Methodist soul over the past generation points us this way. Here is an answer to the important question: Why do we need the Free Methodist Church any longer? Shouldn't we just merge into generic evangelicalism, or melt into mainline Methodism?

Not if we know God's grace and understand our own story. Our identity as Free Methodists is uniquely grounded in our history. What God said to Israel has its parallel with Free Methodism, as for all who have genuinely heard and responded to God's grace: "Fear not, for I have redeemed you; I have summoned you by name; you are mine" (Isa. 43:1).

**Note:** The analysis in this chapter is based on multiple sources in history, sociology, and theology. For ease in reading I have not referenced these sources but have provided a bibliography for any who may want to investigate these matters in depth.

## Bibliography of Sources

Bratt, James D. "The Reorientation of American Protestantism, 1835-1845." *Church History* 67:1 (March 1998), 52-82.

Dayton, Donald W. *Discovering an Evangelical Heritage.* Rev. ed. Peabody, MA: Hendrickson Publishers, 1988.

Dieter, Melvin E. *The Holiness Revival of the Nineteenth Century.* Metuchen, NJ: Scarecrow Press, 1980.

Dunnavant, Anthony L., ed. *Poverty and Ecclesiology: Nineteenth-Century Evangelicals in the Light of Liberation Theology.* Collegeville, MN: Liturgical Press, 1992.

Finke, Roger, and Rodney Stark. *The Churching of America 1776-2005: Winners and Losers in Our Religious Economy.* New Brunswick, NJ: Rutgers University Press, 2005.

Hempton, David. *Methodism: Empire of the Spirit.* New Haven: Yale University Press, 2005.

Hogue, Wilson T. *History of the Free Methodist Church.* 2 vols. Chicago: Free Methodist Publishing House, 1915.

Jones, Charles Edwin. *Perfectionist Persuasion: The Holiness Movement and American Methodism, 1876-1936.* Metuchen, NJ: Scarecrow, 1974.

Kelley, Dean. *Why Conservative Churches are Growing.* Harper & Row, 1972.

Kostlevy, William C., ed. *Historical Dictionary of the Holines Movement.* Lanham, MD: Scarecrow, 2001.

Lamson, Byron S. *Venture! The Frontiers of Free Methodism.* Winona Lake, IN: Light and Life Press, 1960.

M'Geary, John S. *The Free Methodist Church: A Brief Outline History of its Origin and Development.* Chicago: W. B. Rose, 1910.

Marston, Leslie R. *From Age to Age A Living Witness: A Historical Interpretation of Free Methodism's First Century.* Winona Lake, IN: Light and Life Press, 1960.

McKenna, David L. *A Future with a History: The Wesleyan Witness of the Free Methodist Church.* Indianapolis: Light and Life Communications, 1997.

McLoughlin, William G., Jr. *Revivals, Awakenings, and Reform.* Chicago: University of Chicago Press, 1978.

Niebuhr, H. Richard. *The Social Sources of Denominationalism* [1929]. Cleveland: World, 1962.

Oden, Thomas C., ed. *Phoebe Palmer: Selected Writings.* Sources of American Spirituality. Mahwah, NJ: Paulist Press, 1988.

Roberts, B.T. *Why Another Sect.* Rochester, NY: "The Earnest Christian" Publishing House, 1879.

Roberts, Benson Howard. *Benjamin Titus Roberts ... A Biography.* North Chili, NY: "The Earnest Christian" Office, 1900.

Semmel, Bernard. *The Methodist Revolution.* New York: Basic Books, 1973.

Smith, Timothy L. *Revivalism and Social Reform: American Protestantism on the Eve of the Civil War* [1947]. New York: Harper Torchbooks, 1965.

Snyder, Howard A. *Populist Saints: B.T. and Ellen Roberts and the First Free Methodists.* Grand Rapids: Eerdmans, 2006.

Snyder, Howard A. *The Radical Wesley and Patterns of Church Renewal.* Downers Grove, IL: InterVarsity, 1980, and reprints.

Snyder, Howard A., ed. *"Live While You Preach": The Autobiography of Methodist Revivalist and Abolitionist John Wesley Redfield (1810-1863).* Lanham, MD: Scarecrow, 2006.

Snyder, Howard A., with Daniel Runyon. *The Divided Flame: Wesleyans and the Charismatic Movement.* Grand Rapids: Zondervan, 1986.

Stark, Rodney, and Roger Finke, *Acts of Faith: Explaining the Human Side of Religion.* Berkeley, CA: University of California Press, 2000.

Sweet, Leonard I., ed. *American Evangelicalism.* Philadelphia: Temple University Press, 1983.

Synan, Vinson. *The Holiness-Pentecostal Tradition: Charismatic Movements in the Twentieth Century.* Grand Rapids: Eerdmans, 1997.

Wallace, Anthony F. C. "Revitalization Movements: Some Theoretical Considerations for Their Comparative Study." *American Anthropologist,* 58 (April, 1956), 264-81.

Ward, W. R. *The Protestant Evangelical Awakening.* Cambridge, UK: Cambridge University Press, 1992.

White, Charles Edward. *The Beauty of Holiness: Phoebe Palmer as Theologian, Revivalist, Feminist, and Humanitarian.* Grand Rapids, MI: Francis Asbury / Zondervan, 1986.

Winter, Ralph D. "The Two Structures of God's Redemptive Mission." *Missiology,* 2:1 (January 1974), pp. 121-39.

Zahniser, Clarence H. *Earnest Christian: Life and Works of Benjamin Titus Roberts.* Circleville, OH: Advocate Publishing House, 1957.

## CHAPTER 11
# The Free Methodist Soul: Did We Find It?

Bishop Emeritus Gerald E. Bates
Free Methodist Church of North America
President, Spring Arbor University, 2007-2008

I think we did. The issues dealt with by the presenters and the respondents, substantially included in this book, are more than memories; they are live — sure, not uniformly present across the Free Methodist Church, but still dynamic in the composite life of the church. I take these issues, which flow into a kind of untidy consensus, as evidences of a Free Methodist soul, a family identity which has a certain continuity to it across geography, cultures and time.

Take the doctrine of entire sanctification, now more commonly treated as holiness of heart and life, or other terms more reflective of growth and pursuit than status or renunciation or dramatic experience. Admittedly, our ancestors fell into excesses of legalism, at times bordering on works righteousness, but, along with those characteristics, they have to be accredited as *earnest* Christians, willing to sacrifice and set themselves over against the world. One wonders, from our enlightened perspective, if we do as well in terms of passion and sacrifice; if we do as well in drawing boundaries between us and the world? Do our children see boundaries?

I was struck by Mark Van Valin's reference to a Sunday school teacher who wept every time she spoke the name of Jesus. I had one like that, sleeves to her wrists, high-necked dress, long skirt, who frequently wept as she prayed for an unruly class of six- and seven-year-old boys. She had an abusive husband and an unhappy home life, but never missed being there with us to exemplify the joyous Christian life. The point is, she loved us, and we knew it.

Some, I know, profess to be alienated and embittered by the quaint rules and expectations of old Free Methodism. I would not go back to those days, but I have to wonder if we have made a good trade in the replacements we have brought in? The intrusions of modern life do not seem to excite much outrage in us. The fact that I raise this question may be an indication of soul.

> Are we as passionate and as courageous in drawing boundaries between us and the world as were our forebears?

Or consider preaching the gospel to the poor. We admit we don't do it very well, or sometimes very much, but if the issue is dead, why does it bother us? (To be fair, thousands of Free Methodists regularly do acts of mercy and social righteousness.) Why does it keep coming up? An evidence of nascent soul, perhaps? It could be that this question of involvement with our world, both near and far, may rise from our denominational inner depths to do more than inflict us with nagging guilt — perhaps to goad us toward more intentional action.

Another soul facet of our identity is the incurable optimism of grace which seems to keep surfacing over the dispensational pessimism which assails us in much of popular evangelical preaching. Borrowed points of view (and borrowed theology pushed on us by the rapture people, advising us to hunker down while things get worse and worse — "wars and rumors of wars"; hunker down and wait for the rapture — have distracted many of our people and led them from the Jesus (and Wesleyan) perspective which heals, restores, and values — right down here! Bishop Ildo, a voice from the younger church, Brazil, brings us back to hope and the ability to pray the Lord's prayer as Jesus did, "Your kingdom come on earth," not the escape some wait passively for. How Wesleyan! How Free Methodist! How B.T. Roberts with his multiple engagements with justice and the poor.

Bishop Ildo cries out, "The status quo does not have the last word. There is hope!" Is this our soul speaking up?

Following Bishop Ildo in the order of the book is Pastor John Hay's call to "do justice," with the disturbing question, who should do it and where? Perhaps more messages from our soul. Hay suggests, "Theologically speaking, injustice may well be the very irritant around which the pearl of holiness is formed." What a thought!

John Hay mentions the outgrowths of the Free Methodist concern for the poor — higher education, world missions (medical work and schools alongside evangelism), inner-city heroism. Sometimes we have been influenced by an extreme emphasis on personal conversion to the neglect of the Jesus model.

Henry Church, out of 30 years in Africa, says "Mercy is in the DNA of true Free Methodists." He cites International Childcare, ministry to HIV/AIDS sufferers and their families. He concludes: "From the soul of the church comes the gospel of life-changing mercy and pardon, cleaning and cleansing. As long as that message is preached, the church will not lose its soul." More soul talk.

> What will future generations see as our blind spots?

U. Milo Kaufmann points out the enormous task Free Methodists have to actualize their special legacy, "to tell the truth to one another and to *be* the truth, the Good News of Jesus Christ in our world."

The sum of reflection harvested from the three colloquiums (or conversations) exhibits a spiritual longing for depth and passion, and a pragmatic concern with what to do and how.

So — the Free Methodist soul — what are its components? What does it look like (as if we can see a soul)? Howard Snyder suggests we are a hybrid, born of Anglican, evangelical, charismatic and Anabaptist influences. If we accept these as base contributors to our identity we can perhaps understand the effort it takes to maintain the integrity of our special identity in this force field which pulls in one direction or another.

I think I can discern, at various times, the attraction of one or the other of these polarities. However, at the end of the day, many of us feel there is an element of churchly genius in the lively synthesis somewhere around the center. We can even celebrate it, though we find it sometimes hard to explain. The Free Methodist soul has no fence around some exact center. (In fact with the Spirit blowing wherever he wants to, we rather distrust fences.) But somehow in that hard-to-define center we find a meeting place. We trust that our hybrid, or synthesis, comes somewhere close to modeling the richness and complexity (even the paradoxes) we see in Jesus and the Scriptures.

> We have no need to wear others' theological clothes.

This churchly phenomenon of understanding called Free Methodist, in my admittedly biased view, is worthy of publishing, of articulation. I am privileged to hear the message clearly and not infrequently from Free Methodist pulpits today. I love the sense of wonder and discovery of newcomers when they find God in this view and sense that it is right.

We have no need to wear others' theological clothes. If we mime what Jesus brought us — what he taught, where he went, whom he touched, what he denounced — we shall come up with something close to the Free Methodist soul at its best.

Is not that enough?

## CHAPTER 12
# *Our Calling to the Poor*

### Joseph F. James
Bishop, Free Methodist Church of North America
Address given at General Conferfence 2007

"Praise the Lord!

"Yes, give praise, O servants of the LORD.
  Praise the name of the LORD!
"Who can be compared with the LORD our God,
  who is enthroned on high?
"He stoops to look down
  on heaven and on earth.
"He lifts the poor from the dust
  and the needy from the garbage dump.
"Praise the LORD!" — Psalm 113:1, 5-7, 9b, NLT

Jesus said, "If anyone would come after me, he must deny himself and take up his cross and follow me. For whoever wants to save his life will lose it, but whoever loses his life for me and for the gospel will save it" (Mark 8:34-35, NIV).

*The Message* puts it this way: "Anyone who intends to come with me has to let me lead. You're not in the driver's seat; I am. Don't run from suffering; embrace it. Follow me and I'll show you how. Self-help is no help at all. Self-sacrifice is the way, my way, to saving yourself, your true self. What good would it do to get everything you want and lose you, the real you? What could you ever trade your soul for?" (Mark 8:34-37).

Every great movement of God is led by those who deny themselves, take up their cross and follow in the steps of Jesus. These are people who willingly embrace sacrifice, who give up their lives for the gospel. These are people who willingly give anything, do anything, go anywhere ... all for the sake of the call.

Their vision remains clear as long as they keep their eyes on Jesus and live in community with their Lord. The result is real life change, multiplication of disciples, expanding ministries and community transformation.

When Christ's followers take their eyes off Jesus, the call becomes faint, the cross heavy, the road rough and the headwinds discouraging, and the vision goes into a fog. When the first love grows cold, the mission is exchanged for "soft living," little luxuries are substituted for mission engagement, and passion for one more soul is lost. Those who hang on try to preserve the institution. The tragedy is that the poor remain poor; the hungry, hungry; the blind, blind; the prisoners, imprisoned; the lost, lost; and the gospel is silenced.

Hear the passion of B.T. Roberts, founder of the Free Methodist Church, as told by his wife, Ellen. She wrote, "My husband felt we must get a place for worship in the heart of the city, where the gospel could be preached to the poor. He could see no way of doing it except he gave our home towards it. It was all we had. I looked the matter over. We had three children. I thought of the way the Disciples were led, at that marvelous outpouring of the Spirit, when they 'sold their possessions and goods and parted them to all men as every man had need.'"[1]

Then, Ellen exhorted the church: "Let those who have prayed long for blessings not received, begin to feed the poor, clothe the naked, and yield themselves and [their] substance to the Lord as if they meant it, and he will pour them out blessings that will measure beyond their desires and expectations."[2]

B.T. and Ellen Roberts denied themselves, sold their home and established a church in the heart of the city where the gospel could be preached to the poor. The church was soon filled with new life — transformed lives. God honored B.T. and Ellen's yielding themselves and their substance to Him.

When John the Baptist was in prison he wanted confirmation that Jesus was the Messiah. So he sent his disciples to ask Jesus, "Are you the Messiah we've been expecting, or should we keep looking for someone else?" (Luke 7:19b, NLT).

Jesus told John's disciples, "Go back to John and tell him what you have seen and heard — the blind see, the lame walk, the lepers are cured, the deaf hear, the dead are raised to life, and the Good News is being preached to the poor" (Luke 7:22, NLT).

Jesus knew that this would be evidence enough for John the Baptist that He was the Messiah, the One for Whom they had been waiting. Jesus declared that the crowning work of the Messiah was that good news was being preached to the poor.

I am reading through the Scriptures this year. I have been underlining each reference to the poor, or widow, or orphan, or foreigner. I have been noting our Lord's teaching about hospitality and radical generosity. It is amazing how often God reminds us to care about the poor. Why? Because God cares about them. They are important to Him.

In the Old Testament we read the following scriptures: "If one of your fellow Israelites falls into poverty and cannot support himself, support him as you would a foreigner or a temporary resident and allow him to live with you. ... show your fear of God ..." (Leviticus 25:35-36, NLT).

"For the LORD your God is the God of gods and Lord of lords. ... He shows love to the foreigners living among you and gives them food and clothing. So you, too, must show love to foreigners, for you yourselves were once foreigners in the land of Egypt" (Deuteronomy 10:17-19, NLT).

"If there are any poor Israelites in your towns ... do not be hard-hearted or tightfisted toward them. Do not be mean-spirited and refuse someone a loan ... . Give generously to the poor, not grudgingly, for the LORD your God will bless you in everything you do. There will always be some in the land who are poor. That is why I am commanding you to share freely with the poor and with other Israelites in need" (Deuteronomy 15:7, 9-11, NLT).

"Never take advantage of poor and destitute laborers, whether they are fellow Israelites or foreigners living in your towns. You must pay them their wages each day before sunset because they are poor and are counting on it. If you don't, they might cry out to the LORD against you, and it would be counted against you as sin" (Deuteronomy 24:14-15, NLT).

"When you are harvesting your crops and forget to bring

in a bundle of grain from your field, don't go back to get it. Leave it for the foreigners, orphans, and widows. Then the LORD your God will bless you in all you do" (Deuteronomy 24:19, NLT).

"When you have eaten your fill, be sure to praise the LORD your God for the good land he has given you. But that is the time to be careful! Beware that in your plenty you do not forget the LORD your God ... . For when you have become full and prosperous and have built fine homes to live in, and when your flocks and herds have become very large and your silver and gold have multiplied along with everything else, be careful! Do not become proud at that time and forget the LORD your God ... . Do not forget that ... He gave you water from the rock! He fed you with manna in the wilderness ... . He did all this so you would never say to yourself, 'I have achieved this wealth with my own strength and energy.' Remember the LORD your God. He is the one who gives you power to be successful" (Deuteronomy 8:10-18a, NLT).

In the New Testament, John the Baptist told the crowd, "Prove by the way you live that you have repented of your sins and turned to God.

"The crowds asked, 'What should we do?'

"John replied, 'If you have two shirts, give one to the poor. If you have food, share it with those who are hungry'" (Luke 3:8a, 10-11, NLT).

Jesus was back home in His boyhood town of Nazareth. On the Sabbath, as usual, He went to the synagogue. He was handed the scroll and from it He read the words of Isaiah the prophet:

"The Spirit of the LORD is upon me, for he has anointed me to bring Good News to the poor.

"He has sent me to proclaim that captives will be released, that the blind will see, that the oppressed will be set free, and that the time of the LORD's favor has come" (Luke 4:18-19, NLT).

All eyes were upon Him. Jesus told them that Scripture was being fulfilled that very day.

Our Lord's mission is very clear. It is to bring good news to the poor, to proclaim that the time of the Lord's favor has come.

Jesus counseled His disciples with the following: "[Do not] worry about everyday life — whether you have enough food to eat or enough clothes to wear. For life is more than food, and your body more than clothing" (Luke 12:22-23, NLT).

"These things dominate the thoughts of unbelievers all over the world, but your Father already knows your needs. Seek the Kingdom of God above all else, and he will give you everything you need" (Luke 12:30-31, NLT).

> Our Lord's mission is very clear. It is to bring good news to the poor, to proclaim that the time of the Lord's favor has come.

"Sell your possessions and give to those in need. This will store up treasure for you in heaven! And the purses of heaven never get old or develop holes. Your treasure will be safe; no thief can steal it and no moth can destroy it. Wherever your treasure is, there the desires of your heart will also be" (Luke 12:33-34, NLT).

"So you cannot become my disciple without giving up everything you own" (Luke 14:33, NLT).

"If you are untrustworthy about worldly wealth, who will trust you with the true riches of heaven?"

"No one can serve two masters. For you will hate one and love the other; you will be devoted to one and despise the other. You cannot serve both God and money" (Luke 16:11, 13, NLT).

## Three Examples from Jesus

The priority of the poor is expressed in the life and teachings of Jesus. The following three real-life examples are instructive for those who desire to walk in His ways.

The first example is from the life of Zacchaeus — that little man who climbed the sycamore tree, the chief tax collector from Jericho who had become very rich. Jesus made a home visit, and while Jesus was there, Zacchaeus announced to Him, "I will give half my wealth to the poor, Lord, and if I have cheated people on their taxes, I will give them back four times as much!" (Luke 19:8, NLT).

"Jesus responded, 'Salvation has come to this home today, for this man has shown himself to be a true son of Abraham. For the Son of Man came to seek and save those who are lost'" (Luke 19:9-10, NLT). Jesus declared that salvation had come to Zacchaeus' home. Why? There was no "sinner's prayer" here. Our Lord detected an incredible transformation! Zacchaeus was going to make things right with anyone he had cheated. *And* he was going to give half of his wealth to the poor! This is radical generosity. It sounds like John the Baptist saying, "If you have two shirts, give one to the poor" (Luke 3:11a, NLT).

Jesus' response is a stark contrast to the Pharisees who "dearly loved their money" and scoffed at Jesus when they heard Him say, "You cannot serve both God and money" (Luke 16:13-14, NLT).

Surely, salvation *had* come to Zacchaeus' home. Jesus knew it!

Another real-life example is recorded in Luke: "While Jesus was in the Temple, he watched the rich people dropping their gifts in the collection box. Then a poor widow came by and dropped in two small coins.

"'I tell you the truth,' Jesus said, 'this poor widow has given more than all the rest of them. For they have given a tiny part of their surplus, but she, poor as she is, has given everything she has'" (Luke 21:1-4, NLT).

Should we not consider the observation of our Lord in light of the ever-increasing affluence and indulgence of the evangelical church in the West? The Lord may be saying the same of us: "They have given a tiny part of their surplus" (Luke 21:4, NLT). Perhaps this is why there is so little fruit compared to other areas of the world.

Our third example comes from John 13:18-29. Jesus loved His disciples to the very end. The night before His death, Jesus shared a meal with them. We read that during the meal Jesus dipped the bread in the cup and then gave it to Judas and said, "Hurry and do what you're going to do" (John 13:27, NLT).

The disciples assumed that Jesus was sending Judas out to pay for the meal, *or* to give some money to the poor. They assumed this because it was a common practice for Jesus.

Jesus cared about the poor, and *of course* some of the funds they gathered would be given to the poor. The disciples had just enjoyed a good meal. They were full. It made perfect sense to the disciples that now they would give some money to the poor so that they too could have something to eat. Giving for the needs of the poor was a way of life for Jesus and for His disciples.

As we know, Judas did not go and pay for the food. Judas did not go and give some money to the poor. Judas went out and betrayed His Lord for some money for himself!

This crisis moment in the life of Judas is captured in musician Ken Medema's song "Fork in the Road": "Stop right here, there's a fork in the road; one way leads to the potter's field, the other way leads to a cross."[3]

Judas took the road to the potter's field ... and lost his life trying to save it. Jesus took the road to the cross ... and gave His life to save us.

Second Corinthians 8:9 says, "For you know the grace of our Lord Jesus Christ, that though he was rich, yet for your sakes he became poor, so that you through his poverty might become rich."

Psalm 62:10b in the *New Living Translation* summarizes the matter pointedly: "And if your wealth increases, don't make it the center of your life."

Friends, I realize this is a lot of scripture, but I want you to see the litany, repetition and theme that flow from beginning to end. God calls us to a radical generosity toward those in need. God cares deeply about the poor.

### Radical Generosity Is Evidence of Faith

Remember what John the Baptist told the crowd would prove that they had repented of their sins and turned to God: if they shared generously with those in need.

If the evidence of their faith was their radical generosity, it gives me great concern, because when it comes to giving, we are not an obedient people. Oh, we might be doing as well as some other denominations, but Scripture does not make that the standard. God's call is to radical obedience and to self-denial.

The tithe is a biblical baseline for giving. The tithe belongs to God. To do less is to rob God. It is not sacrificial giving. It is not generous giving. It is simply obedience. Yet studies show that typical Free Methodists give on average 3 percent instead of 10 percent.[4]

How does this speak to our care for the poor? Look at it this way. Let's say your church income was $300,000 this past year, and the members are giving 3 percent. If the people gave a tithe, 10 percent, there would be an additional $700,000 in offerings. Not just one year, but every year. Can you imagine the good that could be accomplished if we obeyed the Lord regarding the tithe? Can you imagine the impact in your community and around the world if your church gave $700,000 away in ministry to the poor in your community or your region, or to pressing needs in a poverty-stricken country of the world? Imagine the harvest! That church would be transformed. Jesus would be saying, "Salvation has come to this church."

Studies reported by Empty Tomb conclude that if the evangelical community in the United States would simply tithe, world hunger could be solved immediately.[5] Tithing alone would provide the funds needed to feed the hungry around the world — Africa, Asia, Latin America, everywhere — if the evangelical community simply honored God with their tithes.

> Studies reported by Empty Tomb conclude that if the evangelical community in the United States would simply tithe, world hunger could be solved immediately.

Imagine if every Free Methodist church in the United States committed to give 10 percent of every dollar donated to their building program to a church in a poverty-stricken nation.

What if the people called Free Methodists said, "We are not going to sit in our new air-conditioned, multimillion-dollar facility as long as our brothers and sisters are sitting under a tree, or under a tent, or under a thatched roof. We are Free Methodists. We know that churches are not free. Every seat costs money. We believe that our brothers and sisters in Third-World countries need places to worship just like we do. We will deny ourselves. We will make this a cross-bearing matter, to make it happen, so the good news is proclaimed to the poor. It is who we are. It is our commitment to God's kingdom. We will not move into our new building until they move into their building. We will move in on the same day!"

Jesus would declare, "Salvation has come to this church."

We must never forget that God raised up the Free Methodist Church to reform a church that was in danger of abandoning the poor. God will not have it! The poor have priority with God. We must have the same regard for the poor.

As members of the Free Methodist Church we insist that all seats be free, that the poor are welcome, and that the poor may sit in the best seats in the church if they choose. As members of the Free Methodist Church, we boldly proclaim freedom for all. It was this conviction about freedom that made it unacceptable for anyone to be treated as a slave. The passion of our Methodist founding fathers was, "To spread scriptural holiness across the land and to preach the gospel to the poor."[6] How do we measure up today? Have we forgotten our distinctive calling?

## My Sacred Place at Shadnagar

The church gave me a wonderful gift this past year — a three-month sabbatical. For one-half of my sabbatical I joined Bob Yardy (layman and son of Jessie and Dr. Paul Yardy, founding missionaries of Umri Christian Hospital) and the Reverend John Hay Jr. for a six-week, 2,000-mile bicycle trip in India. It was in support of the poor — to raise funds to rebuild Umri Christian Hospital. It was an amazing experience. I thank God for it.

On a typical day, I was up at 5:30 a.m. I'd wash up, get dressed, read the Scriptures, pray, pack the bedroll, fill the suitcase, fill the water bottles for the bike, lather on the sunblock, spray on bug repellent, and then haul my stuff and bike from my room to the *tata suma* [a jeep]. We'd load the jeep with the luggage, listen to Bob give group instructions, share in group prayer, sip some steaming hot Indian chai, and leave at dawn for a 15-mile ride to a roadside *dahba* [outdoor restaurant] for breakfast.

We left early in the day to avoid the heat and heavy traffic. Our routine after breakfast was to ride 15 miles to a mid-morning break, 15 miles to lunch, 15 miles to a final break, and one more ride to our destination for that day. By then it was hot, about 90-plus degrees.

Gope, the driver of the support vehicle, went ahead of us identifying eating stops and rest stops (in the shade) and locating a cheap hotel for the night.

When we arrived at the hotel, we would haul our bikes and bags to our rooms. Some of the team slept. I liked to clean up from the road dirt and grime.

My "shower" was usually a bucket of cold water with a dipper. Then dressed in fresh clothes, I would take a prayer walk around the town. I'd maybe take a few pictures, find some ice cream, get my shoes polished, talk with the people, hand out a few brochures on Umri Christian Hospital, and be back to my room in about an hour and a half. I'd then download my pictures to the laptop for John to add to the daily blog, read a little, head out for the evening meal, visit with friends and then get to bed.

On Friday, Jan. 13, having completed nearly 800 miles of our 2,000-mile trip, we came to the town of Shadnagar, our destination for the day. The hotel was very basic. I hauled my bike past the front desk up narrow stairs to the second floor and down the hall to my room. The windows were open, no glass, only metal bars with wooden shutters. I placed my bike and belongings along an inside wall where people could not reach through the bars to my belongings. I closed the shutters while I got cleaned up.

When I went to the balcony to see if I could lock the shutters, I discovered the locks were broken. I was feeling vulnerable, and complaining in my spirit about the unsecured windows, the hard bed and the cold water. I was worried that people could walk along the balcony, open the shutters and look in while I was sleeping.

From the balcony I looked across the alley to a vacant lot. I noticed a man standing among some garbage near a round cement culvert that might have served as a burn barrel. He was tall and thin with matted hair that was dreadlock-like. He was wearing a long, ragged shirt, long pants and flip-flops. He grabbed my attention. I stood there spellbound. Without a sound, I watched as he picked through the garbage. He had a small piece of newspaper in his hand, and as he found some food he put it on the paper. After maybe 10 minutes he walked to the edge of the property and sat on a burlap gunnysack in the shade of the neighboring building to eat the food he had found.

> I stood there spellbound. Without a sound, I watched as he picked through the garbage.

Wherever God meets you is a sacred place — holy ground. It is a sanctuary — a take-off-your-shoes kind of place.

I was taken by surprise. Of all places one could call "holy," the balcony of that cheap little hotel in Shadnagar, India, became a sacred place. God was speaking to me. There was no audible voice. But God was confronting me about my attitudes and my expectations. He knew what I was thinking. He was asking me about my complaints: the hard bed, the cold shower, the broken shutters, my requirement for privacy, my feelings of vulnerability. He was reminding me, "I AM with you. I AM all you need."

I stood on the balcony, hushed, looking at a real-life IMAX theatre where the images and the messages were larger than life. I watched the man eat his meal. A cow wandered onto the property, rummaged through the same garbage, ate the same leftovers and then lay down atop the garbage. Men came by the property to relieve themselves since there were no public toilets in the area.

The cow left. The homeless man returned to look through the garbage, but found nothing and wandered back to sit on his burlap couch.

I wasn't sure how to respond. I left the balcony. I went to the main street, found a vendor, purchased a half-dozen bananas and took them to the man. As I approached him, he didn't look at me. Our eyes didn't connect. I reached down and handed him this small gift of bananas. I wanted him to have something nourishing — clean food. I gave the customary bow and a smile. I left quickly because I didn't want to shame him. I didn't know what he was thinking. I didn't know his language. The bike team were probably the only Caucasians in the whole town.

As I walked the streets of Shadnagar that afternoon I prayed for him. Back at the hotel, I was drawn to the balcony again, and there my neighbor sat on his burlap at the edge of the vacant lot.

That evening after dinner, I went back to the balcony just one more time. The man was wrapping himself up in his burlap sack, lying down for a night's rest. That was his address: a vacant lot, across the alley from a cheap hotel in Shadnagar, India. I didn't sleep well that night. I was thinking about his situation. I was thinking about the comforts of my air-conditioned home and soft bed. I prayed for him. I prayed for *me*.

In the morning, I pushed through the routines of preparing for another day on the bike. I took one last look from the balcony. Three pigs were rooting through the garbage, and my neighbor was by the wall in his burlap sleeping bag.

As I biked out of town, I realized I didn't even know his name. Then I remembered the words of our Lord, "… when you did it to one of the least of these my brothers and sisters, you were doing it to me!" (Matthew 25:40, NLT). So I named him "Jesus"!

In the quiet of the morning, in the heart of India, I thanked the Lord for helping me see what He sees every day … the grinding poverty of broken people, the homeless, the helpless, the least, the last in our world. I was so thankful that I serve a God Who cares so deeply and identifies so completely with the neediest in our world.

As I thought about the bananas, I began to laugh. *I sure hope he likes bananas*. It would have been a bad break to give him the one thing he didn't like. I wondered, *Should I have given him some water?*

Gope, our driver, was led by the Lord to choose the hotel. The Lord wanted me to encounter this man at Shadnagar, one of God's cherished missing, *one more soul*. And the Lord gave me a balcony view so I couldn't miss the desperate circumstances of the homeless in our world.

*General Conference attendees entering the evening worship service of July 11, 2007, received a bookmark wrapped in a burlap "sleeping bag." This is the front.*

Notice the scripture:
"He lifts the poor from the dust
    and the needy from the garbage dump"
                          (Psalm 113:7, NLT).

This is the passion of our God. He cares about every person — everywhere.

Notice the background picture from Shadnagar: the vacant lot, the garbage, the cow, and to the right, "Jesus" up against the wall in the burlap sleeping bag.

American essayist Logan Pearsall Smith wrote, "Almost all reformers, however strict their social conscience, live in houses as big as they can pay for."[7] The Scriptures say, "I tell you the truth, whatever you did for one of the least of these brothers of mine, you did for me" (Matthew 25:40, NIV). And, "If any of you wants to be my follower, you must turn from your selfish ways, take up your cross daily, and follow me" (Luke 9:23, NLT).

Perhaps the picture of "Jesus" in burlap will inspire you to deny yourself and invest in the poor in your neighborhood or around the world.

Perhaps the picture of "Jesus" in burlap will convict you about your priorities.

Perhaps it will convict you to take up your cross and carry it to the broken and poverty stricken in the poorest neighborhoods of your city or region or to another nation of the world.

Perhaps it will remind you to pray for those who live and minister in the inner cities and the poorest neighborhoods of our country and the dangerous places in our world.

Our Lord Jesus looks on from Heaven's balcony — saying like God said to Moses, "I have indeed seen the misery of my people in Egypt. I have heard them crying out because of their slave drivers, and I am concerned about their suffering. So I have come down to rescue them" (Exodus 3:7-8a, NIV).

He hears the cries of the neglected poor. He wipes the tears of broken people. He loves the cherished missing with an everlasting love. He cares for the homeless. He embraces the untouchables. He heals the sick. He sets the captives free.

**Our Calling as Free Methodists**

God is calling His people called Free Methodists to share the gospel with the poor.

God is calling His people called Free Methodists to radical obedience, to self-denial, to cross-bearing so we might engage in a vital part of His rescue mission to the lost, the least and the last.

Ray Bakke, International Urban Association founder, writes, "When a Christian moves into a slum, it is a slum no longer."[8]

Donna Saylor, one of our own (Free Methodist urban missionary pastor), says, "I have lived in inner cities for 30 years. I live in the inner city to show God has an inner-city address."

The standard of living in our culture keeps rising. We are a people called Free Methodists. Yet we dress in fine clothes and live in mini-mansions with manicured lawns. We drive minivans, sip expensive coffees, plan resort vacations. We enjoy our little luxuries. They are all nice. It is hard to tell us apart from our neighbors across the street.

Is it possible we are missing out on *real life*, the *radical mission* of who we are truly meant to be as Free Methodists?

I believe we are missing out because we refuse to deny ourselves; take up our cross; and embrace the poor, the stranger, the widow, the orphan and the untouchables of our society.

We're missing out because we can't bring ourselves to move in with Jesus in the alley, to the other side of the tracks, in the inner cities of our nation, among the poorest of the poor in our world.

Lydia Lane helped raise B.T. Roberts' wife, Ellen, in New York City. Lydia had a passion for the poor. Her 1852 diary is full of entries like these: "I visited many poor families [today]." "Had many calls from the Poor." "Today, attended to my poor as usual." "Went after meeting with Miss Maynard to visit a poor sick man, a very distressed family." "[W]ent to visit the family of a Polish Exile. Relieved their wants."[9]

In 2011 the Free Methodist Church anticipates celebrating its 150th anniversary at Roberts Wesleyan College in New York. So we're returning to where it all began. It was in Pekin, NY, where the first convention met under an apple tree and voted to begin the Free Methodist Church.

Imagine the celebration in Heaven, the glory that would be given to Christ Jesus, if we radically followed the leadership of the Holy Spirit in a great revival of bringing the good news to the poor. Imagine if the daily journals of thousands of Free Methodist men and women read like Lydia's journal: "Called on many poor today, relieved their wants."

On the first day of our 2007 General Conference (July 7, 2007), Bishop David Kendall presented the Bishops' Pastoral Address. We responded to the call for repentance and the call to a radical faith to see the fullness of God working among us.

Remember our calling to the poor — as a church and personally.

Renew your confession and commitment to our calling to the poor. Pour out your heart to the Lord.

Respond in your heart to the following general confession. Ask others to join you.

## General Confession

**I/We confess** that I/we have squandered my/our wealth on myself/ourselves and neglected my/our calling to the poor and disenfranchised.

**I/We believe** that God's own heart is especially tuned to the poor and to those who will open their hands to serve them.

**I/We confess** that I/we allow my/our standard of living to be set by my/our culture of comfort and excess, and not the kingdom's culture of radical generosity.

**I/We believe** that I/we can "… be made rich in every way so that [I/we] can be generous on every occasion …" (2 Corinthians 9:11, NIV).

**I/We confess** that I/we have tried to fulfill my/our mission to the poor with meager resources — my/our "leftovers" — and token compassion.

**I/we believe** that miracles of multiplication and provision for the multitudes like the "feeding of the five thousand" occur when God's people courageously give away what they themselves need.

**I/We confess** that I/we have seen holiness mainly in moral terms rather than ministry power.

**I/We believe** that whomever the Holy Spirit fills receives discernment, wisdom, empowerment and resources sufficient to liberate people from physical and spiritual poverty, transforming individuals and whole communities.[10]

Amen.

## Endnotes

[1] Howard A. Snyder, *Populist Saints* (Grand Rapids: Wm. B. Eerdmans Publishing Co., 2006), 502.
[2] Ibid.
[3] Ken Medema, *Fork in the Road* (Word Music, 1972).
[4] John L. Ronsvalle and Sylvia Ronsvalle, "Church Member Giving 1968-2003," chap. 1 in *The State of Church Giving Through 2003* (Champaign, IL: Empty Tomb, 2005).
[5] Ibid., "The Potential of the Church," chap. 6.
[6] Leslie R. Marston, *From Age to Age a Living Witness* (Winona Lake, IN: Light & Life Press, 1960), 13, and Snyder, *Populist Saints*, 258.
[7] Logan Pearsall Smith, *Leadership Devotions: Cultivating a Leader's Heart* (Wheaton: Tyndale House Publishers, 2001), 160.
[8] Ray Bakke, founder, International Urban Association, *Free Methodist Ministries Today* (Indianapolis, IN: Light & Life Communications, Feb. 2007).

[9] Snyder, *Populist Saints*, 53.
[10] Doug Newton, excerpt from "Repent and Believe" (A liturgy of response to the Bishops' Address). 35th General Conference, Free Methodist Church of North America, Spring Arbor, MI, July 7, 2007.

## *Soul-Searching the Church*
# *Study Guide*

This study guide provides a set of ten questions for each chapter in the book. The questions can be used to prompt discussion in a class or small group or as an aid to further personal reflection.

Choose those questions that appear to be most helpful.

## *Chapter 1*
## *Tell the Story: The Soul Importance of Free Methodist History*

1. Is it really important to know and tell (to "rehearse" or "recite") the story of our church? Why or why not?
2. Why does Doug Newton believe it is necessary to tell our story?
3. Is it better to think of our Free Methodist heritage as a history, a set of doctrines, or a story?
4. Are there negative as well as positive things in storytelling? Do *good* stories sometimes include *bad* things?
5. In what ways is the story of Jesus like or unlike the story of the church?
6. Should we know the whole Christian story from the beginning, or only our own part of that story?
7. How well do we know our own local church's story?
8. If we know the story of our own congregation, is it important to know the story of the whole denomination, going back to 1860?
9. Is your own story quite similar to, or much different from Doug Newton's personal story of growing up in the Free Methodist Church?
10. What do you think of the five proposals at the end of the chapter?

## Chapter 2
## *Free Methodist Trajectories:*
## *The Road We Took*

1. What does Stan Ingersol mean by "trajectories"? What is his point?
2. What was Free Methodism's original trajectory, according to this chapter?
3. What does Ingersol mean when he calls Free Methodism a "believers' church"?
4. What is "radical Wesleyanism"?
5. What did you learn about the Free Methodist Church in this chapter that you didn't already know?
6. What is "fundamentalism," and how has it influenced Free Methodism?
7. Is the Free Methodist Church part of the "evangelical mainstream" in America? Should it be?
8. What are the positives and negatives of U.S. culture, as it affects the church?
9. What "trajectory" should the Free Methodist Church take now?
10. Is our church today a reform movement? Should it be?

## Chapter 3
## *Growing Up Free Methodist*

1. What did you find most interesting about Linda Adams' upbringing in the Free Methodist Church?
2. Are there points of similarity between her experience and yours?
3. In what ways might the experience of growing up in the church be different for a girl as compared to a boy?
4. In your experience, has the church affirmed and encouraged women to go into pastoral and other forms of ministry?
5. Many Christians have not grown up in our church because they were converted as adults, or perhaps transferred from another denomination. How can we learn from them? Can their stories help us in some way?
6. Are our roots as a church helpful to us in our own Christian discipleship?
7. What does Adams mean that "at its best, Free Methodism is sacramental, evangelical, radically obedient, and Spirit-filled"?
8. Is it true that as a church we should be "pragmatists"—doing whatever works?
9. Is it possible to "lose our souls by running a church"?
10. In the reflections at the end of the chapter, what does the "Free" in Free Methodist mean especially?

## Chapter 4
## *Embodying Our Mission*

1. What does Van Valin see as most important in the Free Methodist soul?
2. What does he mean by "the pebble in our shoe"?
3. What "two pillars" does he believe support Free Methodist ministry and mission?
4. What should our understanding of holiness be?
5. What is Van Valin's point about "abstinence, status, and separation"?
6. How do we decide what values and behaviors in our culture we should abstain from, actively oppose, or embrace? What does history teach us?
7. What dangers does Van Valin see in a "privatized, isolationist religion"?
8. Should Free Methodists support the Republican Party because it talks about "moral values"? Why or why not? What moral values does the Bible teach? What moral values have been important in the history of the Free Methodist Church?
9. What is Van Valin's point about the direction of Free Methodist financial statistics?
10. In this chapter, what is most important for the life of our local church?

## Chapter 5
## Learning from Brazilian Free Methodism

1. Why does Bishop José Ildo emphasize the kingdom of God? What does "kingdom of God" mean?
2. What is the point of the reference to D-Day in World War II?
3. Do we take seriously enough Jesus' prayer, "May your kingdom come, may your will be done on earth"?
4. Should we be optimistic or pessimistic when we look at the world around us? Why?
5. Could our world today be transformed by the power of the gospel?
6. What aspects of the Wesleyan heritage does Ildo especially emphasize?
7. Should things such as racism and prejudice that divide people in the world also divide the church?
8. How does Ildo define "grace-filled living"?
9. What kind of revival do we need today, according to Bishop Ildo? What do you think?
10. What signs of hope or revival do you see in the church today, or in society?

## Chapter 6
## Free Methodist Mission: Justice

1. How does John Hay define "doing justice"?
2. What place have justice concerns played in Free Methodist history?
3. What is the relationship between justice and a concern for the poor?
4. How should local churches be involved in doing justice?
5. How does the Bible define justice, according to Hay?
6. What is the significance of the verses from Isaiah 58, quoted in this chapter, for us today?
7. What does Hay see as the link between justice and holiness?
8. What examples in Free Methodism of practicing justice does Hay identify?
9. What is Hay's point about fundamentalism? Is he making essentially the same point as Ingersol does in chapter two?
10. How would you evaluate the ways of doing justice that Hay advocates in the last section of the chapter?

## Chapter 7
## *Free Methodist Mission: Mercy*

1. What connection does Henry Church make between mercy and the Free Methodist soul?
2. What examples of mercy does Henry Church point to within Free Methodist history?
3. Are justice and mercy essentially the same thing?
4. What point does Church make concerning the numbers of Free Methodist foreign missionaries over the year?
5. Church says, "We must reach out in merciful compassion if we are to rediscover our soul." Why does he say this? Do you agree?
6. Which stories from Africa particularly impressed you? Why?
7. What do we learn from the story of Langbuoy?
8. In Scripture, what are some of the ways we see God showing mercy?
9. How does our congregation show mercy, both within and beyond the church?
10. Does my life demonstrate the mercy of God?

## Chapter 8
## *Free Methodist Mission: Truth*

1. What "three lenses" does Milo Kaufmann use? What does he mean?
2. What does the "naive observer" see when looking at the Free Methodist Church?
3. What is Kaufmann's point about the language of worldliness and Christian perfection?
4. What does the "partisan" see, and why?
5. What does Kaufmann identify as "core truths" of Free Methodism? What would you add to or delete from this list?
6. What does the "ironic partisan" see in the Free Methodist Church?
7. What does Kaufmann see as a sign of vitality in the Free Methodist Church today?
8. Do you agree that revivalism is largely obsolete today? Why or why not?
9. What does Kaufmann mean by "two distinct modes of staging the Christian life"? How does this relate to your own experience?
10. In what ways are we embodying truth in today's world? How can we do so more effectively?

# *Chapter 9*
## *Reflections and Reactions*

1. What did you find most significant in this chapter?
2. Which of the issues mentioned here are most important to you, or to your church?
3. Is it better for the Free Methodist Church to focus on what makes us different from other churches, or on the things we share in common with all true Christians?
4. What are some of the values and dangers of asking about the Free Methodist soul?
5. What do we learn about holiness from Exodus 3:1–5, according to Bruce Cromwell?
6. Is it true that Christianity is not primarily a doctrine, but a community? If so, what is the significance of that for our church?
7. How does our church embody Free Methodist mission today?
8. What are some ways we can build more effective Christian community?
9. What needs in our neighborhood or city most cry out for Christian witness?
10. What is the place of the sacraments in our life and witness?

## Chapter 10
## *Seven Keys to Free Methodist Renewal*

1. What is the biblical meaning of "soul"? Is this the way we usually think of soul?
2. How did B.T. Roberts and early Free Methodism define the church's mission?
3. What are the four stages of Free Methodist history, according to Snyder? What do you think of this way of understanding our history?
4. What does Snyder mean by the "Free Methodist synthesis"?
5. Where would you (or your family or church) find yourself on the four-sided "map" pictured in this chapter? Where does your congregation seem to fit?
6. What seven keys or steps to renewal are proposed here?
7. Which of these appear to you to be most important or timely?
8. How do these seven proposals interconnect with or relate to each other?
9. What does "mind of Christ" mean? How is the mind of Christ an expression of holiness?
10. In what ways can our church more fully embody Free Methodist mission today?

## Chapter 11
## *The Free Methodist Soul: Did We Find It?*

1. How does Bishop Bates answer the question: Did we find the "Free Methodist soul"?
2. What is Bates' point about "boundaries"?
3. What is the difference between an "optimism of grace" and "dispensational pessimism"?
4. Is your (or our) understanding about what God intends to do in the world through the church essentially optimistic or pessimistic? Is it full of hope, or does it view the world as "hopeless"?
5. What does it mean to "do justice" as part of our gospel witness today?
6. What does Bates mean by "an element of churchly genius" in Free Methodist identity?
7. Is our church really Free Methodist, or does it try to "wear others' theological clothes"?
8. What can our church learn from this whole discussion of "Free Methodist soul"?
9. What are your (or your church's) greatest opportunities for ministry today?
10. If Jesus were mayor of our town, what would he want to do? What *does* God want to do in our town or city or neighborhood that we can be a part of?

## Chapter 12
## *Our Calling to the Poor*

1. What does Bishop James mean by "Our calling to the poor"?
2. On what basis does the author argue for ministry with the poor?
3. What do we learn from Jesus' examples of ministry with the poor?
4. What did Bishop James learn on his bicycle tour of India?
5. Why did he call the poor man he met in India "Jesus"? What do you think of this?
6. How important is the point that the author makes about the level of Christian giving today?
7. What examples does Bishop James cite from the early days of Free Methodism?
8. How does this chapter fit in with the other chapters in this book? Similarities and differences?
9. Is our congregation fulfilling its calling to the poor? What would be some evidence?
10. Do I personally have a calling to the poor? How do I know?